More *fairly* Truthful Tales

A collection of comedy monologues
from the North of England

Written and illustrated by
Gary Hogg
additional material by Stan Brown

Published by
Toontoons

First published in Great Britain by Toontoons 2004

ISBN 0-9544794-1-6

Printed and bound in Great Britain by Proprint
Old Great North Road, Stibbington,
Cambridgeshire, PE8 6LR

British Library Cataloguing in Publication Data.
A catalogue record for this book is available from
the British Library

Published by Toontoons
42 Dunkeld Close
Blyth
NE24 3SP

Also available *'Fairly* Truthful Tales' Book One
'Fairly Truthful Tales' Audio CD performed by Bernard Wrigley
'Amblethwaite 'Appenings' Audio CD performed by Bernard Wrigley

Website www.garyhogg.co.uk

Contents

(Continued overleaf)

Titles marked* written by Gary Hogg and Stan Brown

Foreword

Here we are again! Another hilarious book from the master of comedy monologues. If you're reading this on the bus you'll want to nudge the person next to you and say "Hey listen to this…." That's the secret of Gary's work - it's for sharing. I've had the opportunity to read '*Fairly* **Truthful Tales**' on radio and the response is unbelievable. It's that thrill of entertaining that not all of us get the chance to experience. Learn a couple of these and for years to come your friends will be saying "Do the one about…"

Gary's roots are firmly in the North but the humour is so adaptable. From Glasgow to Liverpool, from London's East End to the Cornish villages, no one is excluded. As funny and compelling as you'd expect from such a specialist, it appeals to all, regardless of geography, age or class.

Although based on a classic style, there is a fresh and unique approach to Gary's monologues. There is a timeless nostalgia incorporated that ensures it will be as popular in fifty years time as it is now.

I can hear things Grandma said and conversations that crossed backyard walls. Things you'll hear from ordinary folk in the Co-op or at the bus stop - but woven into incredible fantasies. His characters are well thought out and his stories structured to get the point across as simply as possible.

A superb follow-up to the first in the series and again, absolutely hilarious. A laugh-out-loud, feel-good book that will make you long for the next one.

Bill Maynard July 2004

Acknowledgements

I would like to thank Bernard Wrigley and Bill Maynard for continued encouragement, undying enthusiasm and support for all my writing.

Grateful thanks to Stan Brown from Oldham who, as a writer of similar material, is always there to offer ideas, constructive criticism and praise. He has co-written some of the items in this book and provided more than a little help with editing.

And to friends Neil Atkinson, Colin & Paul Burke, Ray Hooker, Karis Jones, Tom McConville and Andrew Peel who knowingly or otherwise provided inspiration and help.

To Sandra for her support through the years.

Very special thanks to Jess & Dave Bramley just for being there.

Introduction

Follow-up books, I'm told, are the most difficult to write. This one however, has been a labour of love. The previous book in the series was a collection of writings from several years of unpaid slog, hawked around blinkered publishers and greedy agents before eventually being self-published. This book was written a lot quicker because several hundred happy readers have written to tell me the demand is there. I always knew it would be.

It's good to know that Fairly Truthful Tales are being performed professionally on radio and at concerts but also in schools, lunch clubs, over 60's nights, retirement homes and by after-dinner speakers. And not just in the UK!

Written to complement the very successful Audio CDs produced by Bernard Wrigley, I have eventually succumbed to writing with a nod in the direction of a Lancashire, Yorkshire, Cumbrian delivery. A language known to those in the South or overseas as 'Northern.' Writing dialect is something I had always avoided because I find it so difficult to read if you're not from the area. Spelling words incorrectly doesn't make it any easier for the outsider to pronounce. If you don't believe me, try reading something like 'The Clock Almanack' by John Hartley. It's an excellent taste of Yorkshire but impossible to read if you're not from t'Dales. It's not just Yorkshire writers that do it. A typical example of this is the irritating idea that *Newcastle* sounds more authentic if it is spelt *Newcassel* and Education will be pronounced in true Geordie if written as *Educashun*.

The first book in the series was cleaned up so that Southerners could understand it. However, readers, having heard Bernard Wrigley or Bill Maynard performing, needed help to enable a similar delivery. Although no unnecessary changes have been made to the English language, a few rules have been bent. Be careful because *Hair* rhymes with *Were* in Lancashire. I'm used to *Years* rhyming with *Bears* on Tyneside and rhyming with *Beers* in Northumberland. So what chance has an educated southerner got? Especially if he looks in the rhyming dictionary and finds that *Newcastle* rhymes with *parcel!*

It is quite difficult to recite poetry in Yorkshire or Lancashire accent if it's written in perfect English. Dialect has fewer syllables so- *When Jim Biggins saw the new barmaid in the pub on Saturday night* takes seventeen syllables. Whereas in Yorkshire or Lancashire *When Jim Biggins saw t'new barmaid in t'pub Sat'day neet* it only takes thirteen. This really mucks up the meter of a rhyme and makes it difficult to transpose. The Glottal Stop is responsible for this. Although it's traditional to write it as a *t'* in front of a word it is actually a silent pause produced by stopping the sound from your larynx abruptly, a split second before the next word. This saves you using the word *the*. As we move from Yorkshire to Lancashire where the *h* is rarely sounded and a *th* is used in front of a vowel we get *'e went into th'ouse* or *'e 'ung up 'is coat in th'all.'*

So apart from dropping the odd *g* from the end of *ing*, there's nothing more complicated than that in this book. So have a go. Learn a couple and share them with your friends.

Gary Hogg

A Lesson For Mr Carson The Parson

Mr Carson, the Parson at St. Bob's C of E
Got out of 'is bed Sunday morn'
There were ice on the inside o' t'windows
And a big cloud of steam when he yawned

I remember that winter, the worst one we've had
Minus twenty in t'middle o' t'night
Cold as a well-digger's welly, it were
Nineteen forty-seven, am I right?

We'd frost and we'd snow for three months or so
Roads blocked - folks couldn't get through
Isolated from civilisation we were
I know what you're thinkin' "S'what's new?"

The Parson had slept in 'is long-johns and vest
With 'is jamas on top – nice and snug
His ex-army great-coat on top of the bed
A balaclava pulled down round 'is lugs

He scraped the ice from 'is window and had a look out
The churchyard were covered wi' snow
"There'll be nobody daft enough to worship today,
If I weren't Parson, then I wouldn't go"

He'd 'is duty to do, but between me and you
He weren't too keen, not today
But, a gentleman and scholar, he put on 'is collar
And reluctantly went on 'is way

He'd to dig himself out up the vicarage path
Then dig 'is way in through t'church door
And he knelt then and there for a bit of a prayer
Just to let the Big Boss know the score

"Oh Lord, as thou wilt have read in th'Amblethwaite Post,
We're twenty degrees colder than t'norm,
And there's a slight aggravation of no congregation,
So I'm goin' back home to get warm"

Just then he heard a shufflin' behind him
And he turned and there sat Old Will
He were a shepherd from up o'er yon top side
Who'd spent all night bringin' lambs off the hill

He weren't the full onion, weren't Will, a right funny un
Social skills? No, a bit out of touch
He didn't have enemies, nothin' like that
Just 'is friends didn't like him that much

It were no problem a bit o' bad weather to Will
And he sat in t'front pew all alone
The Parson says "Oh dear, we're the only ones here,
Why don't you and me just go home?"

"Let's call it a day. Go and get yourself away,
To your fireside, your pipe and your chair"
Old Will just sat still, wi' a look that would kill
He says "I've come a long way. That's not fair"

"With respect, Mr C, I'm not clever like thee,
But I know that when my flock's needin' fed,
Come rain, hail or shine, I don't moan, I don't whine,
And I'm up, half past five, out me bed"

"And it's often I'm stood on the fells wi' their food,
…and this bit I want you to heed!
All them yows and them tups - but if just ONE turns up,
I still give the poor beggar 'is feed"

Parson C. were in shock. All that talk about Flocks?
"I'll not 'ave 'im preachin. We'll see!"
He thought "Wi' God's blessin', I'll teach him a lesson,
And a better one than what he's taught me"

So the two of 'em stayed, over an hour they prayed
They stood, then they knelt, then they sat
Singin' hymns till quite hoarse. No organ o'course
And then a sermon for an hour after that

A lot more than he ought "That's him taught" he thought
But says Will, as he bid him good day
"With respect, Mr C, I'm not clever like thee,
But there's one thing I'd just like to say"

"If me flock's needin' fed, I'm into me shed,
And take a cart-load of feed up the fell,
But you have to be fair, if just one beggar's there,
He doesn't get the whole load to himsel!"

Mrs McKie And
The Mysterious Lumps

When Millicent McKie from the W.I.
Come home from her meetin' last week
It looked like a mole had been diggin' big 'oles
And she says to herself "What a cheek!"

So she phoned up the Council, she said "Is that you?"
They said "Aye, whaddya want?" She says "Well,
Can you send someone round to have a look at the ground?"
"What's up like?" ….She says "I can't tell"

"Me front path's all spoiled, there's a big lump of soil,
An' another up t'street, that's not all,
A few yards along, there's some more goin's on,
There's another by t'Vicarage wall"

She were soundin' distressed, so they took her address
And a bloke came around the next day
She showed him the bump, two humps and three lumps
And were concerned as to what he might say

The bloke scratched his head "It's a lump, that" he said
She says "I know" He says "So, what's the prob?"
"Well it's on me front flags" The bloke lit a fag
She says "Well then?" He says "That's not my job"

"Not the Council, ain't that" he sniffed, then he spat
"Someone else's been diggin' that there,
Maybe Water-Board's lads" Well, Millicent went mad
She says "I'm gettin' on t'phone to the Mayor"

He were sat sittin' there, were the Mayor, in his chair
Wi' his hanky tucked under 'is chin
Wi' fish, chips and peas and a mug of hot tea
Knife and fork poised about to dig in

The phone rang, he says "Drat! Who the hell's that?"
"Buggered if I know" says t'Mayoress
They both glared at t'phone. He says "You get it, Joan,
Use yer posh voice" he says "To impress"

"Mayor's residence" says she, like she were chewin' a bee
"It's me Joan" says Mrs McKie
"Do you think t'Mayor's aware of the state of affairs,
Concernin' strange lumps nearby?"

She says "It's Mrs McKie, she's got lumps nearby,
And wants to know if there's summat you've heard"
He says "Tell her to wait till I've eaten me bait,
And I'll try to find out what's occurred"

Well the Mayor were perturbed gettin' dinner disturbed
So he phoned up the Clerk O' The Works
An' he gave him an earful, the Clerk were quite fearful
He says "Hey lads, the Mayor's gone berserk"

So they dashed to McKie's, it were pretty close by
And they checked t'situation at hand
She showed them the bump, two humps and three lumps
An' Clerk O' T'Works consulted his gang

14

"This soils just been dug" said the one wi' big lugs
The little un said "Aye, yer right there"
The big un Sam Wiggin says "But who's piggin' diggin'?"
"Don't know" said the one wi' long hair

So they walked up the road and they met Wilfy Spode
As it 'appened t'were a right stroke of luck
Cos yesterday he'd spoke to a couple o' blokes
In one o' Big Hector Scholes' Bedford trucks

Now, he'd get it in t'neck, would big Hec, if they checked
And he were guilty of what had occurred
But when they got to 'is place, they could tell by his face
He were stressed up to th'eyeballs, he were

An installer of phone poles were Big Hector Scholes
But today he were up to his neck
He were in there alone, he were answerin' three phones
Wi' bookwork all over 'is desk

"I've got five blokes here who haven't turned up!
I'm runnin' the place on me own,
If they're not here the morn', they'll wish they weren't born,
Cos I'll be sendin' the beggars straight home!"

"Instead of three in a crew, I only had two,
Which was all right, or so you'd've thought
But they're hopeless they are, Bert and Alec McGarr,
As much use as a couple o' blokes short"

"Now bein' short staffed, and this might sound daft,
Cos while Bert's good at diggin' of holes,
And Alec McGarr fills 'em in, there you are,
I'm just short of a bloke to plant t'poles!"

Father Tralee And The Infernal Flame

Father Tralee from St Wilfred's RC
Were in t'Chemist's buyin' cream for 'is piles
As he turned to be goin', he saw young Meggie Bowen
Behind him and she gives him a smile

"Halloo, Meggie Bowen, it's yerself, how's it goin?"
She says "Hello Father, fine Father, ta"
He says "Jaze, you look well, lookin' after yoursel'?
You're a picture of health, so you are"

"And how's married life, Meggie, now yer a wife?"
"Oh it's fine Father, nearly a year"
"It's a year? I'll be blessed, you'll have built a fine nest,
And did you have any childer, my dear?"

"Well, - not yet, at least" - "Oh dear me" says the Priest
"Tis a pity but I'm sure they'll soon come,
Now if you take care, and keep sayin' yer prayers,
And Our Lord'll soon make you a Mum"

"You'll have a lift in me car?" She says "Ooh, that's nice, ta"
And just as he dropped her off home
He says "I always drive careful when there's somebody in,
You should be with me when I'm in on me own"

He says "I'm off to a conference in Rome, this next week,
I might even give the Pope a quick call,
What I'll do, while I'm there, is - I'll say a quick prayer,
And I'll light you a candle an'all"

Now just nine months on, Peg the Midwife were rung
"It's our Meggie! Her waters have gone!"
"I'll be there'n a short while, is this the first child?"
He say's "No, it's her husband, I'm Tom"

There were snow underfoot, the electric were cut
And the house were in darkness that night
"Just hang on" Tom said, and he went to the shed
And fetched the old lantern for light

After an hour he had cramp, stood there holdin' the lamp
Meggie struggled then the midwife shouts "Hey,
It's a lovely wee lad, he looks just like 'is dad"
Till Meg turned him up the right way

"Oh he's gorgeous says Meggie" "Hang on there" says Peggy
"Hold that lamp still. We're not done,
It's twins!" Peggy shouts, and Tommy passed out
As she delivered another seven-pound son

She says "…and that's not yer lot. You'll never guess what"
As poor Tom got himself to 'is feet
He says "What?" She says "Look, unless I'm mistook"
And Tom turned as white as a sheet

And there like she said, were another small head
A third boy, she says "Hang on a minute,
"Hold the light low, but Tommy said "No!
It's the light that's attractin' them, innit?"

So they'd triplets that night which suited them right
A whole family in one go, which is nice
But who would have thought an event of that sort
Would happen again to them – twice

Yes triplets, threefold, that's nine kids all told
The local news sent round a crew
But Tom, so I've heard, were a man of few words
And just gave them the benefit of two!

When the Priest next saw Meg, she were lookin' half dead
"Hullo, Father" she said, lookin' stressed
She'd three in a pushchair and three in a pram
And three hangin' onto her dress

He says "Meggie, me love" he says "Heavens above"
As the babies all started to bawl
He says "Jaze! You've got nine, was it triplets each time?"
"No, sometimes we'd nothin' at all"

"They must keep you busy, and yer husband, how is he?
Is he holdin' the fort back at home?
Is he washin' the nappies? He must be so happy"
She says "No, Father. Tom's gone to Rome"

He says "Tom's gone to Rome? What? And left you alone?"
"Er, no, he'll be back in a bit,
He's there on a mission, cos we had our suspicions,
He's gone to blow out that candle you lit!"

Dave The Jackal

Come an' listen to me and I'll tell you a tale
That you might or you might not believe
Of a weird and wonderful occurrence
What some folks find hard to perceive

Now I know the majority of folks round these parts
Can manage from cradle to grave
And have nowt to do wi' a jackal as such
But this tale's about one, - called Dave

Now for them as don't knows, jackals, I suppose
Are wild dogs wi' right sticky-up ears
That live where it's hot, - deserts and whatnot
So you'll not see that many round here

He lived on the outskirts of Cape Town, did Dave
In South Africa where he thought life were dull
Till he went scroungin' in a truck full of apples
And ended up in a warehouse in Hull

Dis-orient-icated, I think is the word
After six thousand miles in a crate
And it took a few weeks wi' just apples to eat
So 'is bowels weren't behavin' too great

Then they set off again wi' him still in 'is box
But he'd chewed through the top and were hidin'
In the hope that he'd be in The Serengetee
But he weren't, it were Amblethwaite Sidin's

When there was no one about he got himself out
Had a right good stretch and a scratch
And set off across Amblethwaite Common
To find a wildebeest or summat to catch

There were nowt but a hedgehog and he couldn't eat that
Then he wound up in Hector Scholes' yard
Where he come nose to nose wi' a rottweiler called Rose
And thought "Flippin' heck! She looks hard!"

The rottweiler were nice, cos she stopped and thought twice
About swallowin' our poor Dave whole
And says "Alright there, love?" then says "Heavens above,
You need a good feed, where's me bowl?"

She says "Here, have some dinner, 'fore you get any thinner,
I could play 'Auld Lang Syne' on yer ribcage"
She says "I like skinny blokes but you're havin' a joke,
Think you'd never been fed since the Ice-age"

With the flame from the Amblethwaite Cokeworks
Reflectin' in t'pond underneath
She looked quite attractive stood there in the dusk
Wi' a sparkle to her eyes and her teeth

She invited Dave to stay at her place that night
A blue Bedford van she called home
And the two of 'em got dead nice and cosy
As snug as two nits in a comb

Now while Rose were quite happy confined to the yard
Our Dave were bored out of his skin
So he went out next day, sayin' "I'm goin' for some prey,
Don't cook owt, I'll bring summat in"

There's not much call for a Jackal in Amblethwaite, tho
There's no gazelles, no wildebeest n'that
No wide desert plains and no pampas nor nowt
Unless you count the spare field by the flats

But he found himself on Amblethwaite High Street
Where the butcher were unloadin' 'is van
So Dave went to ground till there were no one around
And jumped in and done off wi' a ham

Now Rose were that used to eatin' Pedigree Chum
That she didn't take kindly to change
So bein' polite she just buried it that night
And Dave din't think anythin' strange

So once they'd got used to each other's strange ways
And adapted their lifestyle to suit
They lived out their life like husband and wife
And had three lots of puppies to boot

It's sad, I suppose, that poor Dave and Rose
Passed on many years ago now
And though they've long gone, their legend lives on
If you listen I'll tell you for how

You see all dogs in Amblethwaite, be they collies or poms
Chihuahuas, alsatians or pugs
They've all got that sparkle in their eyes and their teeth
And they've all got right sticky-up lugs!

The Day That Jim Biggins Got Conned

When Jim saw t'new barmaid in t'pub Friday night
She were a sight he could hardly believe
She were six-foot in height, with a sweater so tight
That poor Jim found it quite hard to breathe

She'd a right friendly manner, 'er name were Diana
She were blonde and polite and quite bright
Jim'd only come out for two bottles of stout
But he ended up stoppin' all night

He were stood havin' a sup when this feller rolls up
Bought a pint from the lovely Diana
He poured half down 'is throat, then he reached in 'is coat
And plonked a parrot on top o' t'piana

Folks stood there in awe as it wriggled its claws
Then fluttered on down to the keys
Stuck its chest out wi' pride, then it hopped side to side
And played *'Roll Out The Barrel'* in C

Well, folks were dumbstruck, but then he brings out this duck
Which he held up and told folks to "Shush"
And it started to sing, then the parrot joined in
On piana, for *'Old Bull And Bush'*

"Well, I'll sleep in me vest!" says Jim, right impressed
Then the bloke grabbed the duck and turned round
He says "I'm down on me luck so I'm sellin' me duck,
Who's gonna give us five pound?"

Jim were straight in 'is coat, brought out five pound notes
From the pay packet he'd only just got
Then quick as a flash, the bloke picked up the cash
Grabbed 'is parrot and left like a shot

A duck that can sing? Jim needed a gin
He just couldn't believe it were his
He couldn't wait to get home, get 'is paper 'n' comb
And let 'is wife see the duck do the biz

Jim held the duck tight and he bid folks goodnight
With a pride that he found hard to stifle
But to tell you the truth, his Maud hit the roof
…..She were never that good with a rifle

"I've just bought us a duck" She says "Eh?" He says "Look"
She says "A duck?" He says "Aye" She says "Why?"
"It sings songs" She says "Songs?" He says "Aye, sing along,
Get yer banjo, we'll give him a try"

Well the duck, it said nowt. It just waddled about
"You've been done" says his Maud "Flippin' 'eck,
That bloke saw you comin'" "Hang on will you, woman?"
Says Jim "He's just shy, I expect"

But the duck, to this day, had nowt more to say
'Cept once when he quacked at poor Maud
No songs, no nowt, poor Jim had 'is doubts
He'd been victim to a serious fraud

He were right, cos I know, you see that so-and-so
Wi' the parrot, that sold him the duck
Were called Dodgy Hugh. He were bad through and through
And were just out to make a fast buck

Cos 'is piano-playin' parrot were a ventriloquist see
And were just throwin' 'is voice sort of style
But then the plot thickens, cos he used ducks and chickens
Cos the parrot were quite versatile

Not only a ventriloquist but impressionist too
Cos most folks would spot straight away
If he did 'is own squawk instead of duck-talk
"That duck sounds like a parrot" they'd say

They don't prosper, t'be blunt, don't folks that pull stunts
Like Dodgy Hugh did to poor Jim
And he blew all the money on the horses, it's funny
It were the same day 'is parrot packed in

It were the night before Christmas an' no food in the house
When off its perch the parrot just dropped
No more dirty tricks, Dodgy Hugh felt quite sick
Cos 'is income had suddenly stopped

So when Jim and his Maud sat down Christmas day
To roast duck, - a lovely big fresh 'un
Hugh had taties and carrot and a seven ounce parrot
That were doin' a turkey impression!

When Cyril Dropped Dead
For The First Time

When Cyril Waggot dropped dead for the first time
His wife Queenie, right enough, were quite shocked
Well she would be, you see, he were just eighty three
But "He's dead as a haddock" said the Doc

Now Queenie, being Northern and not one to fuss
Says "Eh, never mind. That's that"
And she set off to th'Amblethwaite Co-op
To get a black coat and black hat

He were laid out in t'bedroom by Mrs Nextdoor
A dab hand at layin' out she were too
Always doin' a good deed when folks were in need
Not that folks who were in need ever knew

Now I don't know if you know but down Gimmers Row
The houses are all kind of small
They were built back in t'seventeenth century
When they didn't make folks quite as tall

They'd a tiny front door, straight onto the street
Back yard with a privy and that
With the ceiling's dead low, there's no headroom, you know
Cos in those days they never swung cats

The front lobby were narrow, with a piano parked there
And the landin' all cluttered wi' stuff
The undertaker Stan Stokes nearly had a stroke
Getting' the coffin back out - right way up

Him and his lad, Fred, heaved it up round their heads
Just then Stan shouts out "Ooh, me back"
He let slip and the coffin come flyin' downstairs
And gave the piano a right flamin' crack

The piano struck a chord as the lid slammed shut
It were enough to waken the dead
In fact, so I've heard, that's just what occurred
Cos Stan shouts out "Hey, listen Fred"

31

When the dust settled down and they picked themselves up
They heard this quite eerie like moan
It were comin' from inside the coffin
And poor Fred said "Sod this. I'm off home"

So Stan had a listen and aye, right enough
He heard a scratchin' and moanin' inside
So he got out his penknife and prised off the top
And there were Cyril sat rubbin' his eyes

Stan stood there amazed. Amazed and quite phased
Thought he'd best give the Doctor a shout
So he came and he said right enough he weren't dead
Cyril says "That's champion, now can I get out?"

They helped him out the coffin, he were feelin' right stiff
Maybe not quite as stiff as he should
But a quick glass of grog and a visit to t'bog
He were startin' to feel pretty good

The Doctor were asked to explain things
Cos both Cyril and Queenie weren't chuffed
"You'd no pulse nor nowt. Usually means you checked out
Unless me stethoscope's bunged up wi' fluff"

So they don't know what happened but he soon felt quite well
'Fact he lived for twelve year after that
And his missus had to give back the insurance
But the Co-op wouldn't take back the hat

Aye, twelve more years poor Queenie had to abide
Cos as a husband he were never that good
Always boozin' and gamblin' and round-the-town ramblin'
And rollin' in drunk for his grub

So the next time he dropped dead it looked fatal
Just how fatal though the Doc wouldn't say
Not till he'd got second opinions
From the Midwife and the Vet, Mr Gray

So there came the same bother when the coffin had to leave
Stan Stokes just thought "Oh Flamin 'eck,
I remember this staircase from last time,
It were here that I nearly broke me neck"

So this time he got six big strong helpers
And passed the coffin right carefully down t'line
With Queenie stood there at the foot of the stair
Shoutin' "…and mind that piano this time!"

The Warburtons'
Disappearin' Waistcoat

He were always fair game for the Nit-nurse young Graham
He carried all manner of bugs
"You're filthy" she shouts, as she dragged the lad out
"And have you seen the insides of your lugs?"

It's not just poor Graham, 'is whole family's the same
A right lot of scruffy old louts
His dad, Cain's a strange chap, he must sleep in that cap
There's not many seen him without

Now their annual fortnight to Skeggy came up
Same guest-house they went every year
A right home-from-home. Full o' lice like their own
Run by big Aggie Bartlett it were

She were ugly Big Aggie, wi'out abusin' the word
Not blessed wi' good looks that's for certain
Even pervy old Pete, the peepin'-tom 'cross the street
Once asked her to close her front curtains

Cain and Mabel arrived wi' the bairns, half-past five
Their holiday clothes seemed quite new
Ma in t'new frock, young Graham in new socks
One red and the other one blue

Pa wore the waistcoat that Mabel had knit
In bright yellow, he felt a right toff
With 'is jacket pulled wide and 'is chest out wi' pride
He says "Folks here'll think we're well off"

That first night on the prom as they sheltered from t'storm
Ma said "Cain, I'm sure you'll agree,
Before we go home, next Sat'day but one,
You must go for your dip in that sea"

He says "Aye Ma, yer reet. It's good for me feet,
And me back. It's a miracle cure,
For all aches and pains an' if it weren't for the rain,
I'd be in there right now. That's for sure!"

It were persistent, the rain, so it seemed odd that Cain
Despite lightnin' an' the odd thunderclap
Were bare-headed that night, he says "Too flamin' right!
I'm not sittin' in th'ouse wi' wet cap!"

But next day he were bad, a sore throat's what he had
"I'd best not go swimmin' this morn'"
Ma said "That's okay, there's still thirteen days"
And Pa didn't look too forlorn

Next day, it were queer, Pa had this bad ear
"It's me lug, Ma. It's got us reet worried,
Best not go in t'sea" …Ma says "I agree,
There's still twelve days left, there's no hurry"

Now you'll never guess what, but next day were red hot
Says Pa, as they went for a stroll
"I can feel me 'ead spinnin', I'd best not go swimmin',
I think I'm comin' down with a cold"

He'd sniffles and coughs for ten days, on and off
But the Friday before they went home
He'd run out o' complaints, though he felt a bit faint
When he realised he'd have to brave the foam

He could put it off no more, so while Ma sat on t'shore
Pa went paddlin' in up to 'is neck
Ma gave him a wave, she thought "Ah, in't he brave?"
As pa thought to himself "Flamin' heck"

The bairns, Graham and Jane swam out to meet Cain
And they helped the old lad back to shore
He were happy he were, it were nigh on a year
Before he'd have to do that any more

It were next day he noticed 'is waistcoat had gone
"I know where it is! It's bin nicked!
When I were in t'briny, some light-fingered swine, he,
Must've come and done off wi' it quick"

And from that day there, he never saw hide nor hair
Of the waistcoat that Mabel had knit
Until last day of t'fortnight the followin' year
When he went to t'same place for a dip

He come runnin' up the beach as pink as a peach
"I've found it!" and he let out a cheer
Mabel were sat in her hat, she says "Ooh, fancy that!
Must've been lyin' on the beach for a year"

Well that's what she thought, but it were nowt o' the sort
He says "I bet you would never have guessed,
Last year, it were when, I put me clothes on again,
I'd gone an' put it on under me vest!"

Walter West And His Denture Adventure

There's a conductor works on the eighty-eight bus
From Amblethwaite up to Mill Trough
He's called Walter West, and the bit he likes best
Is tellin' folks where to get off

He's not blessed wi' good looks, isn't Walter
He hasn't got a tooth in his head
It's handy, I suppose, for lickin' 'is nose
But not pretty when he's eatin' 'is bread

His speech isn't that clever neither
When he has to shout "Shix sheatsh inshide!"
He sucks 'is gums for a bit, he's all dribbles and spit
But really, the bloke's got no pride

Mind he wouldn't hurt a fly, wouldn't Walter
In a fight? Not worth a candle
Shy and subdued, so it were a bolt from the blue
That night when he flew off the handle

He'd got in from work and sat down for 'is tea
Ma had been boilin' a knuckle
The bairns were both there, Priscilla and Claire
Ma looked and she started to chuckle

Cos Walter were reachin' for the big pickle jar
Right on the very top shelf
She knew what-were-what but Walter'd forgot
Eatin' pickles left a mess down himself

"Pickles?" she says "You'll be needin' yer teeth,
You know that pickles don't melt,
Go'n get them" she said, "They're in the jar by the bed"
So he shot off upstairs at full pelt

It were where they belonged but, there they were gone
Not a sign, just a jar full o' watter
He jumped up and down, started clashin' around
Ma shouts up "Hey! What's the matter?"

"Itsh me falshers!" he yells, "Have you had them yershel"
She shouts "No, not since last Sunday,
I borrowed them when Jock brought that big stick of rock,
But I give you them back first thing Monday"

He searched drawers full o' socks and the back o' the clock
And he groped down the sides of the chairs
He searched all about, turned the house inside out
Even the cupboard under the stairs

He checked the tea caddy, the sewin' machine drawer
Coal hole and rabbit hutch too
He'd a look in Ma's bag, nicked a couple of fags
But the pickle still never got a chew

He looked in the tater bag, the shoe cleanin' stuff
The pockets of 'is old de-mob suit
Inside the piano and 'is box full of spanners
Even shook out 'is Wellington boots

In the yard he were found wi' the bin upside down
You could see nextdoor twitchin' her nets
The bairns went and hid when he chucked the bin lid
Don't think they'd ever seen him so vexed

It were gettin' on for ten when he gave up the hunt
Sat on the step, glum as a trout
He'd been suckin' that pickle best part of four hours
And decided he'd best spit it out

The followin' morn Ma were makin' the beds
After Walter had set off for work
There under the pillow of the youngest, Priscilla
Walter's gnashers were sat with a smirk

She thought for a while as the gnashers just smiled
Then shouts "Priscilla! Here, make it snappy"
She bounced in all a-clatter like nowt were the matter
But could see that her ma weren't that happy

"Come on, our Priss, what's the meanin' of this?"
The lass stood without even a blink
Calm and composed, she just says "Oh, those?
They're for the tooth fairy, who do you think?"

She's a feisty young lass, like her ma, bold as brass
She pointed at the gap in her gob
She says "If I got a tanner for just one of these,
Then that lot'll fetch fifteen bob"

When Joe Gow Went To Hell By Mistake

Our teacher Miss Blair, with the long nasal hair
Were ugly and fat and quite short
She'd bruises where blokes must've give her a poke
Wi' bargepoles or summat o' t'sort

There were a bangin' at t'back of our classroom one day
"Who's makin' all t'noise?" shouts Miss Blair
She couldn't quite see but a voice shouts "Just me!"
And a hand started wavin' in th'air

"Well whoever you are, you're in detention tonight"
"But I can't, Miss" said the voice "Don't be cruel"
She says "I'll not have you crashin' and bangin' an' bashin',
You can stop back tonight after school"

"But, I'm meetin' me mates" said the voice "Down the pub,
And after that there's a poker game on!
I've to get home, get dressed, cos I'm in a right mess,
So I can't hang about for too long"

Well Miss Blair got a scare, she just flopped in her chair
He says "Please Miss, I'm just doin' me job"
"You're stoppin' late!" He says "But I'm t'plumber's mate,
I'm just here fixin' radiator knob"

Miss Blair felt right daft and all the kids laughed
As t'plumber finished and packed up 'is tools
Slung 'is bag over t'shoulder "That's fixed it" he told her
She just blushed cos she felt such a fool

That were fifty odd years ago, summat like that
But that plumber, I'll never forget
And if he hadn't passed on, Pancake Tuesday, just gone
He'd be fixin' folks' radiators yet

Now he should've gone straight up to heaven, you see
But somehow some wires got crossed
And even though he were regular on Sundays at church
He didn't get to meet the big boss

But Satan were right pleased to see him, down there
He said "Come in, Mr Gow. Sit thee down,
I understand that you once were a plumber?"
"I still am!" said poor Joe wi' a frown

"That's grand!" says Old Nick "Cos I'm gettin' right sick,
Th'air-conditionin' keeps goin' on the blink,
It's so flamin' hot with all these fires we've got,
Could you have a quick look, do you think?"

Meanwhile up in Heaven it had gone ten past seven
St Peter were checkin' 'is book
"I'm tellin' you" he says, to 'is helper, Big Les
"There's someone gone missin' here, look"

He double checked 'is list and delivery slips
Says St Peter "We're one angel short,
There's a plumber called Gow, should've been here by now,
Hope nowt's 'appened that shouldn't've ought"

"It's gettin' quite late. Go and stand at that gate,
Long masses? They shouldn't be allowed"
"But I cannot see nowt" he gave Big Les a clout
"Go and see if he's got stuck in them clouds"

So Big Les picked up t'list and disappeared into t'mist
And were gone for an hour or more
He came back really chewed with 'is wings soakin' through
Sayin' "I've been right back down to t'ground floor"

He'd not seen hide nor hair. St Peter's stood there
Scratchin' 'is halo and rufflin' 'is wings
"I can think of one place, we'd best check just in case,
You'd best give Old Horny a ring"

So straight away Big Les picks the phone up and says
"Aye, It's me. Who's that? Is that you?"
And the voice down the line says "It's quarter past nine,
You're up late, are you havin' a do?"

"I'll have less of yer cheek you little pipsqueak,
Have you a new lad down there name of Joe?"
"Who? The plumber, Joe Gow?" he says "Aye he's here now,
Been busy solderin' this last hour or so"

"Well you've no right to keep him, I say, you've no right,
We want him despatched here first class"
"You got no chance," says t'Devil, "The lad's stoppin' here,
He's managed to turn down the gas"

"He's a godsend" says Nick. Les says "Don't take the Mick,
You can't keep the lad there it's a sin"
He says "Oh, shut yer gob! I'm ME! That's me job,
Pick yer harp up, put down t'violin"

"But we need a plumber we've had a gas leak since summer,
You can't keep all the best ones down there"
St Peter grabbed t'phone, breathin' fire and brimstone
And shouts "Send the lad up, that's not fair"

"We'll sue!" He says "Who?" He says "You" He says "Ooh"
He says "I'm goin' to give t'lawyers a call,
The Boss'll be cross" ..Nick says "I don't give a toss,
All the best lawyers are down here an'all!"

Ruby Ruddick's Bad Knees

Ruby had just done the dishes and made all the beds
Swept the front path, the yard and back stairs
You know Ruby Ruddick down Bolsover Street?
She's the one with the budgie that swears

She'd just finished scrubbing the step out the front
On her knees as she did every day
When along comes old Cissie, purveyor of gloom
To tell her who'd just passed away

The latest, Mrs Whatsit, were a hundred and two
When she turned up her toes, Monday night
She asked Ruby if she were going to the funeral, next day
She says "No, I believe you, s'alright"

It were when Ruby stood up to give the step a bit swill
That her knees just sort of give way
She says "Ooh, flippin heck!" and then hit the deck
And Cissie just stood there dismayed

"That's just the way me Mam went" said Cissie, dead sullen
One minute fine then the next she's flat out
Ruby says "Aye," as she mopped herself dry
"But she'd drunk twelve bottles of stout"

"It's just housemaids-knee you silly old B"
She'd never had much time for Cissie
Since the two were at school, she'd thought her a ghoul
And were always so prim and so prissy

"Aye, me Auntie had that, she didn't live long"
Said Cissie "Me poor Auntie Anne,
God rest her soul" Ruby says "Who Annie Scholes?
She got knocked down by the Library van"

She couldn't be chums wi' someone so glum
So she chased her saying "Get lost, you old bore,
Go and visit the hospital, that'll cheer you up"
And with that she slammed the front door

And she hobbled on through to the parlour
Using her mop as a crutch
She says "That come in handy" as she poured out a Brandy
That she kept for occasions like such

They're getting worse are these knees but she had to agree
She were better off than poor Auntie Peg
Cos a crocodile, you see, took a shine to her knees
She ended up wi' two wooden legs

She were fine till that night she set the chip pan alight
They had to get the Fire Brigade round
The parlour weren't too badly damaged, thank God
But poor Peggy got burnt to the ground

"I'm not that bad yet, I've still got the full set"
Said Ruby taking the weight off her feet
The Doctor called the next day, the budgie shouts "Go away!"
But he used language I couldn't repeat

The Doc had a bit prod and she gave him the nod
When he touched the bits where it felt queer
"It's me knees, can you see, they're as sore as can be"
He says "Aye, I can feel it from here"

She says "I'm in awful pain. Is it a break or a sprain?
D'you think you'll be able to mend it?"
Then he lifted her leg up and says "Bend your knee"
She says "Which way d'you want us to bend it?"

"It's nothing to worry about, now Ruby" he said
"At our age we all start to creak"
He says "What'll be best, is just plenty of rest,
Oh, and don't climb no stairs for a week"

He gave her a prescription for painkilling pills
And again he said "Don't climb no stairs!"
Then he left her with her feet on the pouffe
Confined to her fireside chair

Leonard the lodger came in, he'd to go to the shops
Make his tea and then wash up the pots
He'd to do his own washing, make his bed for a week
And at housework he wasn't too hot

Old Cissie called round just to see if she'd died
But she didn't get past the front door
And Joey the budgie shouted "Go and get lost!"
Plus some things I can't say, 'cos he swore!

But Ruby were no better 'fact she felt ten times worse
The Doc were puzzled and just scratched 'is head
"If you'd took advice to the letter, you would've been better,
But you haven't been resting them" he said

Ruby says "You've known me for a lot of years now,
You give advice and you know I don't shun it,
But you said, then and there, that I shouldn't climb stairs,
Climbing that drainpipe every night -that's what's done it!"

The Amazing Mahatma From Clegg Road

Bill Bendelows from Co-op haberdashers
Were takin' in t'blind Friday night
When he heard his name spoke, and there stood this bloke
Stood grinnin' and dressed all in white

He says "Well, I'll be blowed, Seth Sykes from Clegg Road"
Seth says "Aye, but I'm not any more,
You're looking at the Amazing Mahatma,
The Psychic from a far distant shore"

"Far distant shore? You used to live just next door,
Like I say, on Clegg Road, number five,
Din't you once do an act wi' a dummy?
Ventriloquist like, am I right?"

"Yer spot-on" says he "But between you and me,
I'm not into that any more,
Like I say I'm the Amazing Mahatma"
"Aye, you said….. From a far distant shore"

"Well that's just a gimmick to make us sound cool,
Mysterious an' sort of aloof"
Bill says "You must have some loot, an' what's with the suit?
You look like a right flamin' goof"

"That's me image. And aye, I'm doing right well,
Come on and I'll buy you a half,
And I'll tell you how I made all me money"
Bill says "I'll just get me cap and me scarf"

Seth clicked his fingers and a car drew up close
He says "We'll go in the Rolls, we're not walkin'"
"And we're not drinkin' halves, not wi' you dressed like that"
Says Bill "Don't want folks to start talkin'"

The chauffeur pulled up at the Amblethwaite Arms
And ushered the old pals inside
Where they ordered two pints and two pasties
From a bloke who were fat and cross eyed

"So what's this you said about *physics?*" asks Bill
"Psychic, man! Psychic!" says Seth
"I'm a clairvoyant, I can see in to t'future,
And talk to folks after their death"

"How the heck did you ever become one of those?
You were throwin' yer voice last I knew"
He says "I don't rightly know but one night doing t'show,
It sort of came to us out of the blue"

"I'd gone as far as I could - I were pretty damn good!
I even played in front o' t'Royal Highness"
"Oh, aye" says our Bill, who were smellin a rat
"I know you were big on the wireless"

Seth says "I know it sounds funny but now I get money,
For putting folks in touch wi' the dead,
I can get them to talk to their Grannies"
"How the hell d'you do that then?" Bill said

"Well, for a fiver, I contact your friend who's passed on,
It's quite a perplexing technique,
An' for a tenner you can ask him, well, owt that you want,
And for fifteen I'll get him to speak"

"You must be rolling it in" said Bill wi' a grin
"That's cos I'm top o' me league,
It's me speciality you see, that bumps up the fee"
"What's that then?" says Bill quite intrigued

"Well, say some woman's right glad to talk to her Dad,
And I get Dad to talk back to his daughter,
But this time around for an extra five pound,
......I'll drink a whole glass full of water!"

An Elephant's Foot For The Hall

Eighteen inches it were but it caused a right stir
When uncle Jimmy come back from Bengal
He'd got Bridget a prez. "What is it?" she says
He says "An elephant's foot for the hall"

"I'm not havin' that, no way, an' that's that,
A dead foot? The bugger'll stink"
"It's harmless enough, it's been mounted and stuffed"
She said "Hey, wash your tongue in that sink"

He said "How do you mean?" She said "You're obscene,
One track mind"   Jim says "Flippin' heck,
It's just an elephant's foot, it's supposed to bring luck"
She says "I'm not wearin' that round me neck"

He says "Just give it a rub, see if it does any good"
She says "See?" He says "What?" She says "You,
Have you got no respect? Always on about sex"
And she belted poor Jim with her shoe

She were like that, 'is wife, 'ad been all their life
Always knockin' poor Jimmy about
So any chance that he got he were off like a shot
"I'll send you a postcard" he'd shout

He'd bring a memento from places he went, so
It'd stop her from smellin' a rat
A straw donkey from Spain, a rug from Bahrain
And from Moscow a nice winter hat

There were a transistor wireless he got from Hong Kong
A Ming vase all the way from Taiwan
From Holland a clog, and a hand-carved pot dog
From a market in Azerbaijan

He were a sailor, he reckoned. I could tell in a second
He weren't. He were just a big cheat
All the tat that he brought, were just stuff that he'd bought
At Sid's junk shop on Bolsover Street

Cos between you and me, he'd not been to sea
All 'is talk about ships were just joshin'
He were stayin' you see, with the widow McFee
And came home once a month with 'is washin'

And each time he did he'd pop in and see Sid
To see if he'd got owt bizarre
From a far distant land, just to have in 'is hand
And to say to 'is wife "There you are"

But frigid old Bridget would just stand and fidget
"Oh aye," she'd say "What's it this time?"
And he'd tell her a tale, to where he had sailed
He were spot-on at spinnin' a line

He'd tell her all sorts, about far away ports
Of the storms as he rounded the Horn
The warm scented breeze on the South China Seas
While she were just stood daggers-drawn

She'd get 'is washin' all done and dried in the sun
Or up the laundrette if t'weather weren't good
She'd help pack 'is case and with a reluctant embrace
She'd get shot as quick as she could

His shore-leave complete he'd skip off up the street
And back to 'is jezebel's arms
Leavin' 'is innocent wife to her puritan life
Wi' not the slightest of cause for alarm

But what he din't twig, was she weren't such a prig
Not as righteous as what she let on
Extremely frustrated, she sat there and waited
Until she were sure that he'd gone

With some gin from the shelf she'd compose herself
Then sit and put on her slap
Then get dressed in her splendour, frilly suspenders
And them stockin's wi' seams up the back

Then in her prettiest of frocks she'd pop down t'phone box
And make a quick call to Sid's shop
He'd say "Alright, me dear?" She'd say "Aye, t'coast's clear,
Get yourself round here, chop-chop"

So without any fuss he'd be on the next bus
And as he sneaked in the door at the rear
She says "I don't want to niggle, were you havin' a giggle?
Get that elephant's foot out of here"

"And when he comes in to spy for his next alibi,
Could you just give him summat quite small?
You know sort o' thing, like a sovereign ring,
Not an elephant's foot for the hall!"

So that's where it sits with all Sid's other bits
Waitin' for its day of glory
To perhaps catch the eye of some passer-by
But I think that's a whole different story

The Lion, The Witch And The Warburtons

Cain and Mabel were hidin' behind the settee
Cos the rent man were at the front door
When Cain noticed summat under the skirtin' board
That no one had noticed before

He whispered to Mabel "Look at that, Ma
There's a light shinin' through from in there"
"That's a right funny biz, last in t'street, this house is,
Through that hole should be nowt but fresh air"

So when the rent man had gone Pa says "Now hang on,
I've always thought this room were small,
When you look from outside, it looks fifteen foot wide,
But in here, it's nine foot wall-to-wall"

"There's six foot gone astray" Ma says "Get away!
A secret room behind t'wall is that right?"
"Well ain't that peculiar, fetch our Graham's ruler,
He were sword-fencin' with it last night"

So they measured within and they measured without
Right enough they found six foot not there
"I know what I'll do" Pa says "I'll knock through,
I'll make a hole just behind that there chair"

It took an hour an' a bit until he could fit
His head and 'is shoulders right through
An' there sat this witch wi' a wart on her snitch
She says "Y'aright?" He says "Fine thanks. Are you?"

She says "Oh, can't complain, I'm just bored out me brain,
Day in and day out doin' nowt"
"Who you talkin' to?" shouts Mabel, who were still only able
To see Cain's back end stickin' out

It were then that Cain noticed he weren't in a room
He were deep in a forest o' sorts
From what he could tell, it were a green leafy dell
"It's likely enchanted" he thought

Wi' birds all a'twitterin' he din't hear Mabel witterin'
As he bundled the rest of him through
The witch patted the grass, she says "Company at last,
Sit down lad. I've just made a brew"

She says "I have to admit, since t'last folks done a flit,
And took that old wardrobe away,
We've not seen a soul until you made that hole"
She says "Eeh, lad. You *have* made my day"

"Wait I'll fetch Brian" she says "Brian's me lion"
And she got up and shouted 'is name
Right enough she weren't lyin' cos this lion come flyin'
Thank goodness the bugger were tame

He curled up next t'Cain. He says "Ello, what's your name?"
He says "Cain, I'm t'bloke from nextdoor"
You could see he'd been cryin' had Brian the lion
"Eeh, it's right nice to see you" he roared

"Me and t'witch are right lonely. We keep thinkin' if only,
We had visitors, that'd be great,
Cos you see, me and her, like enemies, we were,
But now there's just us, we're best mates"

Just then Cain heard a yelp and what sounded like 'Help!'
It were Mabel t'were shoutin' poor soul
She'd got sick of waitin' but were now suffocatin'
She'd got herself wedged in the hole

A right frockbuster were Mabel she weighed twenty stone
Cain looked and says "Heavens above!"
She were stuck halfway through and turnin' quite blue
Round the gills, so he give her a shove

Course the wall gave way and the witch shouts "Hooray!
We're free!" Mabel says "Hang about,
What's 'appenin' our Cain, I don't want to complain,
But in't that a lion got out?"

"This is Brian" said Pa "…Brian, this is Ma,
And this here's a witch I've just met"
And the witch says "It's right nice to meet you"
And Mabel says "Cup o' tea, pet?"

So the witch and our Mabel sat down at the table
The pair hit it off really well
She gave her some make-up to hide all her warts
And then, …she taught Mabel some spells

So everythin's rosy and they all live quite cosy
Wi' a curtain cross the hole that were made
They don't do Skeggy no more, they just nip nextdoor
And relax in their own verdant glade

So the Warburtons still live life as normal
'Cept wi' a lion instead of a dog
And there's just them in t'street got a forest en-suite
Oh, and a rent man that's been changed to a frog

Doctor McSweet And The Mysterious Noise

I remember the Bank Holiday charabanc trip
That were t'night we got home to no lights
There were a power-cut you see, so there weren't no TV
Folks went to bed early that night

So poor Doc McSweet that lives up our street
The private houses up top and on t'right
Come t'followin' May, he were deliverin' all day
And he were still out deliverin' all night

Cos the Midwife, old Peg, were off with her leg
And Amblethwaite's not got a reserve
So poor Doc McSweet, he were run off 'is feet
Wi' a lot more than what he deserved

So, after deliverin' about twenty four babes
In twenty four hours he were whacked
And even though it were middle o' t'mornin'
He decided he'd best hit the sack

He were asleep as 'is head hit the pillow
But it weren't long before he awoke
Cos there were a rattlin', sort o' buzz at the window
Like a pig crunchin' a sackful of coke

Well he lay half asleep sort of wonderin'
If it were some sort of trumpetin' phantom
Were it a low flyin' plane or the truck suckin' drains
Or t'telegram boy's BSA Bantam

It were a bit like a chainsaw cuttin' through 'is front door
Or the farmer drivin' pigs up to market
Or t'travellin' shop, mebbes th'exhaust had come off
And he were lookin' for somewhere to park it

It were a bloodcurlin' sort of a raspin' like roar
Like one of them Baskerville hounds
Or Farmer Green's muck-spreader clearin' its pipes
Like a flatulent hippo-type sound

He thought mebbe it were thunder but pretty close by
Like a growlin'-type-grumblin'-type rumblin'
Or someone sawin' wood in 'is attic
Or a fifteen-stone bumble-bee bumblin'

His curiosity at last got the better of him
And seein' as he weren't goin' to sleep
He thought he'd get up, put 'is dressin'-gown on
And go to the window and peep

He didn't know what he'd find, so he took a deep breath
'Cos the noise were beginnin' to scare him
His teeth clenched right tight and 'is knuckles wrung white
There were nothin' that could have prepared him

'Cos he opened the curtains, saw this bespectacled face
Snorin' through a wide open gob
It were window-cleaner, Stan Brown, a bloke well renowned
For fallin' asleep on the job

This time he were at top of 'is ladder, spark out
Wi' 'is nose against t'window he stood
And 'is bucket and shammy just danglin'
He were snorin' like a rhino in mud

"I'll not knock" thought the Doc "Case I give him a shock"
The whole thing were best treated wi' caution
He didn't like to wake him 'case he jumped and fell off
So he thought he'd best take some precautions"

He got t'cord from 'is dressin' gown, fastened Stan's hands
To the radiator inside which were near
Then he went down and snuck up behind him
Gently whisperin' in Stanley's right ear

Well Stan started gigglin' 'cos he were dreamin' you see
About their Sandra gettin' all sorta lovin'
She had him tied up, while she nibbled 'is ear
And massaged 'is shoulders wi' dubbin

He were just about to turn and give her a kiss
When he woke and saw Doctor McSweet
And for a second or two he were puzzled, it's true
As were the forty-odd folks stood in t'street

The Doc got him down and examined him like
Said "You'd best get off home for a rest,
Just leave t'windows and go" so Stan yawned "Righto"
As he polished 'is specs on 'is vest

Well it were less than an hour and the Doctor's phone rang
It were Stan's Sandra creatin' a din
"Stan's been sat sittin' there, asleep in 'is chair,
Wi' 'is gob open, ...and a mouse has run in"

"I don't know what to do, he's goin' all blue"
"I'll be there in a tick!" the Doc shouts
"But in the meantime, wave some cheese in front of 'is gob,
Just to see if you can coax t'beggar out"

He were there in ten minutes but couldn't believe 'is eyes
With the sight that greeted him there
There were Sandra stood wavin' a kipper about
And there were Stan, wi' gob open, in t'chair

"What the hell are you doin' wi' a kipper?" says t'Doc
As poor Stan looked like he might burst
Sandra, turnin' red, shouts "I know what you said,
But I've to get flippin' cat out there first!"

Re-incar-thingummybob

It were two top-coats warmer than the Costa del Packet
On the day of the Sunday-School trip
"Yippee!" shouts young Bob "The beach! Just the job,
I'll take me cozzy, mebbes go for a dip"

It were a charabanc ride down beside the seaside
Where they'd sarnies and home made sausage rolls
There were a fairground where Bob won a goldfish
By hookin' a duck wi' a pole

Now as wi' most functions to do wi' the church
There's a bit o' religion chucked in
And they'd to sit and sing hymns and hear stories
'bout what were good - and like what were a sin

There were a discussion 'bout reincarnation come next
He were astonished were Bob, right gobsmacked
That some folks who died just stayed dead for life
But others got the chance to come back

But they din't always get back as people, as such
Sometimes they'd just have to make do
Wi' comin' back as dogs or as rabbits or frogs
Kangaroos or shrews or gnus

So Bob got to thinkin' on the bus ride back home
Just how much he missed Granda Mac
Poor bloke passed away just last New Years Day
It would be right nice to have him come back

It were then that he noticed 'is goldfish sat there
Which kept openin' and shuttin' its gob
And anyone half decent at lip-readin'
Could see it were tryin' to shout 'Bob'

Bob nearly passed out but he didn't say nowt
Till he got home and had a good gander
And aye, right enough - he wasn't half chuffed
The fish even looked like 'is Granda

He shouted "Yippee! - Hey Mam, come and see,
It's happened just like what I wished,
It's him, Granda Mac. He's gone and come back,
And this time around he's a fish!"

His mother come runnin' to see what were up
"It's him! It's me Granda" shouts Bob
"It's yer what?" says 'is ma. He says "Look! It's yer pa!
He's been re-incar-thingummybob"

Mam weren't convinced but she had a bit squint
And she humoured the lad and said "Aye,
Well there's one way to tell" she says "Here, move yersel,
See if he still likes a bit shepherds pie"

She put a big dollop down into the bowl
And it landed with a sort of a squelch
The fish swallowed it whole, did a victory roll
Wagged 'is tail and then let out a belch

"That's yer Granda alright" said 'is Mam, turnin' white
She sat down cos her legs had gone wobbly
She says "I know it sounds whacky – but I can smell baccy,
Yer right, he's come back, I think ....probbly"

And from 'is bowl sat on top of the piana,
He sat listenin' to the day's football scores
When he heard 'is team won he flapped 'is tail and he spun
And splashed water all over the floor

Now at t'bottom of 'is bowl there's a tunnely thing
What fish like to swim through or hide
And all of a sudden he dived in and hid
Cos he'd just noticed summat outside

It were Mrs McGrath comin' up the front path
'Course Granda couldn't stand the old trout
He used t' nip off and hide in the shed there outside
But this time he couldn't get out

So he stayed out of sight for the rest of the night
And seemed happy enough on the whole
And the next couple of years they got on just fine
Until one time he jumped out the bowl

He jumped from the top o' t'piano that day
And he landed on t'keys with a splat
As dead as a filleted flounder he were
Just between C sharp and E flat

Well Bob were dead sad when he came in from school
And he buried him that night in the yard
But he knew that someday he'd be back here again
Just findin' him were gonna be hard

But he never stopped lookin' from that day till this
Cherishin' all of God's good creations
He wouldn't tread on a bug or a snail or a slug
In case it were someone's relation

Now it's funny how things happen like out of the blue
Cos Bob reckons he's found him again
It were strange how it happened it were two women yappin'
In the Co-op when Bob got the gen

There couldn't be any doubt, cos that silly old trout
Mrs McGrath'd had got a kitten called Ted
Who eats shepherds pie and keeps nippin' outside
And spends most of its life in the shed!

Jim And Maud's Separate Lives

Jim Biggins and 'is Maud had become a bit bored
Got into a sort of routine
They'd forgotten the nice things they once liked to share
Stagnatin' if you know what I mean

They weren't always so glum, like the day when they won
A thousand on the Premium Bond
Jim promised 'is wife "It'll not change our life"
But he'd no clue about what lay beyond

With The Goons in full flight on the wireless that night
Either side of the fire they were sittin'
Him and 'is pipe and 'is dog sat at one side
And her at the other side, knittin'

Then she says "Oh, to pot!" she says "Jim, you know what?"
He says "What?" She says "I've just been sat thinking"
He says "Have yer?" She says "Aye, I think we should buy,
A new carpet for in here. This one's stinking"

"It's that dog, It stinks!" He says "Oh, do you think?"
As the dog rolled on 'is back like a rhino
"And your dirty great boots, you don't give a hoot,
You've got the beggar worn through to the lino"

He looks and says "Where?" She says "There by your chair"
He says "Oh!" She says "See?" He says "Aye,
It's not too bad isn't that, we just need a new mat"
She says "It's wall-to-wall we're gonna buy"

"And you need a new chair, you've worn that threadbare
We'll have a new couch while we're on,
And some curtains and nets" He says "Steady on pet,
I'll miss this old chair when it's gone"

Maud thought, then she said "Stick it out in the shed,
You can sit there when yer havin' a smoke"
He says "Eh?" She says "Aye" "Out there?" he says "Why?
In the shed? You havin' a joke?"

"You're not coming in here with that dog, never fear
Yer fag ash, and 'is hairs on the floor,
And one thing's for certain, yer not stinkin' the curtains,
And muckin' the place like before"

"And this wireless is knackered. All Christmas crackered,
A radiogram, that's what we'll get,
Have that for the shed" Jim were scratchin' 'is head
He says "Well, thanks a lot, pet"

So when the new stuff arrived poor Jim felt deprived
Him and t'dog sat outside every night
While Maud were in there, sat in HIS brand new chair
"All that money? It's not worth a light"

But he got the old rug, made the place nice and snug
The old curtains hung up for the draughts
With a paraffin stove and the wireless "By jove!
That's me self sufficient!" he laughed

Meanwhile Maud were indoors admirin' her floor
Sittin' there in the new Parker-Knoll
With the curtains draped wide she were grinnin' wi' pride
'Case the neighbours were out on patrol

Every night Jim bought chips on the way home from the pit
And him and the dog did just fine
Fact he didn't see Maud till one night he were bored
And nipped down the pub, half-past nine

He'd just ordered a round and some crisps for the hound
And turned round to talk to the lads
When he saw Maud sat sittin', in the snug with her knittin'
All alone and she looked proper sad

He felt sad himsel' as she reached for the bell
To order another small stout
"I'll get that!" shouts Jim, and he carried it in
Sayin' "Hey up, Maud, what's this all about?"

She took a quick sup and then she filled-up
"It's us two" she sobbed "It's not right,
Forty years we've been wed and there's you in yer shed,
And me on me own every night"

"You said money wouldn't change us. You promised us,
But it has and I've about had enough"
He says "Come here buggerlugs" and he gave her a hug
And the dog snuggled up and said "Wuff"

They kissed long and slow, like that day years ago
When they'd kissed for the very first time
He looked in her eyes "Walk you home?" She said "Aye"
"Just a minute though! ….Your place or mine?"

Half A Crown A Week

There's a tailor called Gubbins down Bolsover Street
Makes suits and sells stuff off-the-peg
Got a right big posh sign, wi' *'Bespoke'* underlined
So he can charge folks an arm an' a leg

Winnie Biggerstang were studyin' the window one day
She weren't wantin' nothing too bright
Her husband were goin' to a funeral that week
It were his own, so he had to look right

Now Gubbins weren't one to miss out on a sale
He dropped his needle an' came out from behind
He could tell at a glance he were in with a chance
Of robbin' the poor lass blind

He dragged her inside, he were beamin' wi pride
Like a cat wi' some sort o' disease
He says "These ones are nice" She says "Not at that price,
Summat not quite as flash, if you please"

His grin didn't go it just faded a bit
"Certainly ma'am, this one here,
This one's twelve guineas" "Twelve guinea?" says Winnie
"I don't think I've made meself clear"

Then she noticed a notice hung up on the wall
That Gubbins didn't want her to see
It said *'Suits for hire'* She says "Might I enquire,
Just how much a hire suit would be?"

"For a week? Half-a-crown" he said with a frown
"That'll do nicely" she said
"That pin-stripe looks best. He's a forty-six chest,
And about twenty-eight inside leg"

She popped straight round the Co-op, brown parcel in hand
"Can you put our Bruce in this here?"
The undertaker, Stan Stokes, just said "Okey doke"
She says "I just need a quick word in yer ear"

She says "I know it sounds rash, but he left us no cash,
So I had to get that suit there on hire,
When he goes behind curtain, can you make flippin' certain,
That you take it back off before t'fire"

"No problem" says Stan "I'll tell the Crem. Man"
And he did, to be fair, I were there
But he just pushed the buttons, so he told Fatty Hutton
He's the feller who gets 'em prepared

Now it's noisy in there and to this day Fatty swears
That he heard him say "Take off 'is boots"
So when Winnie collected, she hadn't expected
Just his ashes, his clogs, and no suit

She didn't know what to say to old Gubbins t'next day
She just paid half-a-crown and left sharp
She didn't dare to let on that his hire suit had gone
Up to heaven with her Bruce and his harp

Months and months it went on and the two became fond
Of each other and their meetin's each week
When she went into town to pay half-a-crown
He were mystified by the mystique

They become quite good friends and one day that back end
Outside it were blow'n up a storm
Cold enough for two pair o' shoelaces it were
So he invited her through to get warm

They got on okay and they pass'd time o' t'day
Talked o' t'weather and stuff, like you would
She thought it were grand when he asked for her hand
And they married as quick as they could

They've been married ten years now have Gubbins and Winn
And it seems that the pair are in clover
They get on all right, part from him bein' tight
An' turnin' t'gas off while she turns an egg over!

And she still hasn't told him what happened to t'suit
And where you an' I would think it a cheek
He thinks nothin' funny, from her housekeeping money
Of still takin' his half-crown a week

Jack And The Beansprouts

Masie Orrick had just buried their Horace
And she said to her son "Listen Jack,
He's left us no brass, so we'll have to eat grass,
And that telly'll have to go back"

They were smallholders with a very small holdin'
They'd no need for a tractor or plough
In fact all they'd got, were a ten-by-ten plot
Six rows of spuds and a cow

She says "Them taters'll have to see us through t'winter,
And poor Daisy might fetch a few quid,
You'll have to take her t'market on Thursday"
So the very next Thursday, he did

He'd not been gone long when he met Mister Wong
The Chinese lad - owns t'chippy up t'street
He says "By 'eck, ruvvery cow. You give him me now,
I give you prenty beef cully to eat"

"He's a her" says our Jack, givin' daisy a smack
Cos she were chewin' at Mister Wong's welly
He says "Give us food every day from now till next May,
And a fiver to pay off the telly"

"You dlive a hard bargain" the Chinaman said
And from 'is wallet he peeled off a bluey
He said "You bling the cow and I give you now,
First flee meal - king plawn chop-suey"

"Champion" says Jack. He couldn't wait to get back
And tell 'is ma 'bout the deal he'd just made
She weren't chuffed, as it 'appens and gave him a slappin'
Then chased him down t'street wi' a spade

The chop suey got chucked out o' t'window
She'd to start peelin' taters instead
And Jack, he got nowt, cos she locked the lad out
And he 'ad to spend t'night in the shed

Now the chop suey it landed on the compost heap
And it started to sprout overnight
Next morn there's a beansprout a hundred foot high
So big that it blocked out the light

Jack couldn't believe it – he squinted 'is eyes
Then he thought he'd best climb up it quick
Cos he heard 'is mam shout and then she came out
And she were wieldin' a dirty great stick

He soon disappeared from out 'is mam's reach
And climbed till he were right up in t'clouds
He saw a little bloke there, like stood on a chair
Who were screamin' and shoutin' dead loud

"I'm the giant! I'll kill yer!" - Jacks says "Yer a what?"
He says "I'm a giant" Jack says "Yer too small"
The giant says "For a start, I'm quite big round these parts,
So just watch it or I'll eat you an' all"

Jack says "You're not a giant" He says "I am too,
I'm a great ogre and they call me Big Kevin"
Jack says "Well how come, you din't fee-fi-fo-fum,
And you're only about three foot eleven?"

Kev says "You needn't talk you cheeky young gawk,
Yer hardly Charles Atlas yersel,
You need a good clout! Yer what? Four stone nowt?"
Jack says "I know, but I haven't been well"

"Since dad popped 'is clogs we've had a right flippin' job,
No food an' no money or owt,
You should try eatin' grass" He says "No thanks, I'll pass,
You think you've had it bad? Well that's nowt"

"You should try eatin' beansprout like I have to do,
And a brew that's made out of sprout juice,
You see me brother's away doin' the pantos,
And he left me to look after the goose"

"You've a goose?" says young Jack, quite taken aback
"You'll have plenty of eggs you can eat"
"Huh, not this stupid goose. It lays eggs that's no use"
Says Kevin "You'll just break yer teeth"

"Wow, these eggs are gold" says Jack "Get em sold,
Yer rich. Why not go to the shops?"
"There's no shops up here, no pubs no beer,
Gawd I'd kill for a nice big pork chop"

Says Jack "Right, here's a plan. You come meet me Mam,
Sell some eggs and we'll all take a share,
And we'll all live like Lords, you'll have free bed and board,
Bring the goose and we'll keep it down there"

So Kevin and Jack and the goose all went back
Down t'beansprout where Masie meanwhile
Had watched 'em descend an' said "Ooh, who's yer friend?"
And she straightened her curlers and smiled

It were love at first sight in spite of 'is height
And 'is tights and 'is curly toed shoes
And she found him a lot more attractive
When Jack told her all of 'is news

They lived happy ever after did Masie and Kev
Once they'd chopped down the beansprout n'that
In case 'is brother should decide to climb down it
To find out where Kevin were at

They swapped Daisy for three tons of beansprout
Which Mister Wong won't get through in a hurry
Thereby savin' the poor cow from a fate that somehow
Befalls cows that are destined for curry

Joey Ruddick's Bad Language

You must've heard of Joey Ruddick from Bolsover Street
The most foul-mouthed little budgie you've seen
And you can't blame poor Ruby who owns him for nowt
Reg'lar churchgoer - and she always has been

Every morning she takes off his cover
Blows a kiss and says "Hello my sweetheart"
But Joey just gives her a one of his looks
And says "Nick off, you ugly old fart"

She gets really upset cos she loves him so much
But it's embarrassin' if anyone's there
And she's tried all manner of remedies and cures
But never seems to get anywhere

She's tried teachin' him hymns and nursery rhymes
Makes him listen to Radio Four
But he's just learned a few posher swearwords
And some that Ruby had not heard before

Now you can't blame poor Ruby for getting annoyed
It's enough to send most round the bend
And there's times that her patience has just sort of snapped
She's done things that they don't recommend

Like the times that she's acted un-Christian like
Out of character, for Rube, so to speak
She'd been threatenin' for a while that she'd wash out his gob
So soapy water once, she shoved down his beak

There was once she got angry, dragged him out by the throat
Cos he'd been singin' rude songs just to tease her
"I'll show you who's boss"… He says "I don't give a toss"
So she stuck him in the back of the freezer

But then she felt awful as soon as she'd done it
And she took him straight out, kissed him better
It hadn't hurt him nor nowt, he was just trying to work out
What that chicken must've said to upset her

Now most mornin's Joey looked out the window
And swore at the folks walking by
There were once he said "Sod off!" to the Parson
And the Parson poor lad, nearly died

He couldn't believe what the budgie had said
But forgave him and went on his way
But the very next morning he shouted the same
And the Parson were shocked, you might say

But being polite, he thought he'd best just say nowt
Getting angry wouldn't do any good
He just give a bit shrug put his fingers in t'lugs
And hummed "Jerusalem" as loud as he could

Ruby wasn't aware of these strange goings on
She were usually in t'scullery out back
So Joey was free to do owt that he liked
And carry out his verbal attacks

There was one day last Easter, she came down in the morn'
Took the cover off his cage like you would
And when she opened the front Parlour curtains
Mr Carson the Parson were stood

She quickly threw the cover back over the cage
She was scared of what Joey might say
And a voice from under the cover shouts out
"That were a short bloody day!"

She chucked her pinny in t'drawer and went to the door
He says "Sorry to trouble you, dear,
But yer budgie keeps shouting abuse at us like,
And what he's sayin, you don't want to hear"

"Cos I'm just on me way to the station, you see,
To meet the Bishop who's coming to stop,
I'll be walking back past in about half an hour,
He'll think yer budgie's a bit over the top"

So Ruby apologised as best as she could
Closed the door and come back in a rage
And she grabbed hold of Joey by the scruff of the neck
And dragged him right out of his cage

She says "Right, you little beggar, I'll sort you this time"
She got the black sticky tape from the shed
And she wrapped it dead tight round poor Joey's beak
And up round the top of his head

So he sat on his perch dead miserable like
And with the little bit strength he had left
He started scowling at folks as they walked past the house
And mumblin' under his breath

So it was all nice and quiet when the Parson walked past
With the Bishop just like what he'd said
All bound and gagged, Ruby silenced the lad
So he just stuck up two fingers instead

The Pontificating Chauffeur

When Stan Stokes had a win on his Premium Bond
He went and got a skinful o' beer
He smacked his boss in the gob, then said "Stick yer job"
He'd been wantin' to say that for years

He left t'Co-op, where he'd been, since the age of fifteen
As a Funeral Director / Embalmer
And t'next month, every day, he whiled time away
Sat at home drinking tea in his 'jamas

One day, Kath his wife, said "You're wastin' your life,
I'll not have you sat sittin' there,
Just lazin' about, day in an' day out,
Shift yer feet, Stan. An' get out o' me hair"

"So we've got a few bob, but you still need a job,
Set up on yer own if you can,
You're the best that there is, in the funeral biz"
"That's a crackin' idea, that!" says Stan

So that's just what he did. He spent fifty quid
And got him an old hearse for starters
It were in pretty poor nick, an old Austin Six
In which someone'd been growin' tomatoes

So while Kath hoovered out, our Stan set about
Doin' t'king-pins and sortin' the clutch
He fit two exhaust brackets and adjusted the tappets
And a paint job just t'add final touch

Then he picked up a Bentley it were forty years old
"But for now" Stan just thought "It'll do"
A coupla new tyres, course the tax had expired
In March nineteen fifty two

It needed patches on t'floor, a decoke and re-bore
Been lyin' on a farm full o' hens
Kath got rid o t'muck and polished it up
An' our Stan were in business again

Kath had her doubts about layin' folks out
In the shed, but she weren't one to moan
On the very first day, they'd a call right away
So Kath went to answer the phone

"Stanley Stokes, Undertaker and Embalmer" says she
"That Stan?" She says "No, it's his Kath"
He says "This here's the Pope" well Kath nearly choked
"The Pope? Are you havin' a laugh?"

He says "No love, it's me, I've a problem you see,
And I'm told your Stan could help out,
I've just been for tea at St Wilfreds RC,
And the strangest of things' come about"

"Had me bike nicked off t'path" "Don't do bikes" says Kath
"I know, but you don't get me drift,
I've a plane to catch home, the 5.30 to Rome,
D'you think Stan could give me a lift?"

"Well I don't rightly know, just hang on a mo,
I'll go and have look in his diary"
And Stan, who were sat, says "Who the hell's that?"
She says "Shut up it's a chauffeur enquiry"

"Not a hen-night, I hope" She says "No, it's the Pope"
"The Pope?" and Kathy says "Shush!"
She says "We've one car spare, don't fret, he'll be there"
Pope says "Great, cos I'm in a right rush"

Stan picked up the Pope. He says "You'll drive fast I hope?
If I miss getting home I'm in trouble,
Go faster, man, Stan" "I'm goin' fast as I can,
Thirty limit and I'm doin' near t'double!"

"That's only fifty eight, I'm gonna be late"
He says "Pull in and let me bloody drive 'er,
Sit in t'back o' car …and here …have a cigar,
I'll drive and I'll pay extra fiver"

The Pope got in t'front seat and set off up the street
Doin' ninety as they passed the bank-top
They hit a loose grate and they lost t'number plate
And neither of 'em saw the Speed-Cop

It were young Robbie Cropper the motorbike copper
He caught 'em and made 'em pull in
When he saw they'd no plate he moaned "Oh, aint that great"
He just stood there and rubbed at his chin

They looked right important so he thought he best oughtn't
Do owt till he got t'Sarge on t'phone
Wi' a tremble in 'is voice "Sarge, I've stopped a Rolls Royce,
I think they're important he groaned"

"It's not a Rolls, it's a Bentley" says the Pope "Incidentally,
It's not my car, it's his in the back"
The sarge shouts "Tek care, is it t'Mayor you've got there?"
He says "No! …. more important than that!"

"Not Prime Minister then?" Robbie looked once again
He says "No it's a bloke wi' a cigar,
I think it's some one quite high, and I'll tell you for why,
You'll never guess who he's got drivin' the car!"

Ethel And Charlie And Peg And Her Fred

Now the Sidebottoms, Ethel and Charlie
Lived just at the end of our street
Right clever and posh the pair of 'em were
Wore shoes and not clogs on their feet

He'd a right good job had their Charlie
Sat sittin' all day at a desk
While Ethel 'is wife she didn't do much
Just made sure he had on a clean vest

She didn't even do that if the truth's to be told
She didn't do bugger all, lazy mare
'Cept makin' sure that she spent Charlie's wages
And drivin' t'poor lad to despair

They'd a woman for washin' and ironin'
An another for blackin' the grate
And one that came in to polish and dust
And maybe just peel the odd grape

Now Charlie weren't allowed in the parlour
She said he'd just trail in his muck
He'd the hall and the landin' the bog and 'is bed
And the kitchen if he had to wash-up

When he told me, I said "You are kiddin'?"
"No, she's a right fussy bugger" he said
"Why only last week she had me wipin' me feet,
Without socks before I got into bed"

"I wouldn't mind it" he said "If she worked hard herself,
But she just sits there like, all high and mighty,
Spread out on t'settee with a big box of chocs,
And there's some days she's still in her nightie"

Now there's only so much that poor Charlie could stand
And a bright idea came into 'is head
So now he's hardly in there to dirty the place
Cos he went out and bought him a shed

He's put it right at the far end o' t' garden
Backin' on t'the folks o'er t'back
And he's up there most nights with 'is slippers and pipe
The wireless, a flask and a snack

Now you might think it's co-incidental
But Peg the Midwife were in the same boat
If she ever sets foot in her parlour
Her Fred nearly goes for her throat

Cos he's sat in t'peaked cap wi' a whistle
And 'is train-set's laid out on the floor
So poor Peggy has to sit in t'back kitchen
And pass 'is dinner through an 'atch in the door

So one day when she were hangin' out t'washin'
She saw Charlie out paintin' 'is shed
And the two of them just sort o' got talkin'
And she told him about her husband, Fred

So he let onto her about Ethel n'that
They'd so much in common they had
That they talked for an hour, it might've been three
She thought Charlie were such a nice lad

And Charlie thought she were a bit of alright
And he invited her in for a brew
She said "Eeh, this is right nice and cosy"
So she went out and bought a shed too

Now there's two sheds there stood back-to-back helpin'
To restore Charlie and Peg's self-esteem
It's where Peg takes her knittin' and Charlie sits sittin'
Quite innocent or so it might seem

But there's a connectin' door o' which folks don't know
And now Charlie and Peg are an item
Sat there every night cuddlin' up nice and tight
While Fred plays trains ad-infinitum

And while Ethel, oblivious, sits with her Milk-Tray
Indulgin' her unsocial habits
Her Charlie and Peg are up in their sheds
And the pair of 'em's at it like rabbits!

Connie The Conductress

She were a conductress were Connie from just out our back
Which I think's a bit flippin' frightenin'
Cos when I say a conductress I don't mean on a bus
I mean the sort that gets clattered by lightnin'

You see it's summat to do wi' these magnetic storms
Which most folks would give a wide berth
But not Connie Gray, she keeps getting' in t'way
And attractin' th'electric to earth

Now it happens so often that she don't bat an eye
"Water off a duck's back" lass'd say
I don't know about ducks but the last time she were struck
She walked wi' a waddle t'next day

T'were a lot bigger'n before and it left her quite sore
And she felt a bit down in the mouth
She were all magnetised, you could tell by her eyes
Cos one pointed North, t'other South

Now me? I'd be scared, but she were prepared
And she had a quick ratch in her bag
And fished out these forty watt light bulbs
That she kept with her aspirins and fags

Now I know it sounds daft but what worked in the past
Was a lightbulb screwed into her gob
Then she'd plug one, right snug, into each of her lugs
And she discharged herself, just the job

It were normally quite quick, the dischargin' bit
But this time it took most of the night
She'd to get out of bed and go walking instead
Cos she just couldn't sleep for the light

It had gone three o'clock, she were half way round t' block
When t' park gates suddenly gave a loud crack
Cos they found her allurin' and broke from their moorings
And come flyin' and stuck to her back

She'd suddenly become quite attractive you see
Trouble is, it were only to metal
And t'nightwatchman, poor soul were just mindin' his hole
When off flew his brazier and kettle

He nearly swallowed 'is teeth, he shouts "Hey you. You thief!
I need them for makin' me brews!"
Then some grids by his side just started to slide
And so did he, cos o' t'toecaps in t'shoes

The knocker-up bloke, that's big Norman Stokes
Were on his bike when he lost all control
And he ploughed into Connie, the gates and all that
She shouts "Watch where you're shovin' that pole!"

"Hey you! Get off!"…He says "Can't" She says "What?
C'mon and stop acting the goat"
But her right fist were attracted to the brace on his teeth
And she knocked four or five down his throat

Well it looked a right sight in the middle o' t'night
Connie, Big Norm and his bike
The night-watchman, his grids and a few dustbin lids
A red hot brazier, a kettle and t'like

Face to face the three stood wi' Big Norm spittin' blood
And makin' a gurglin' sound
But if that weren't enough along came Bill Clough
The milkman just starting his round

He were still half asleep, in a dream, so to speak
When he spotted Connie, the gates and the blokes
Rubbed 'is eyes to see clearer, and watched 'em slide nearer
And stick to the side of his float

He says "Get off me truck" She says "I can't cos we're stuck,
Magnetic like" He says "What?" She says "Aye"
Then without any warnin' they were joined by an awnin'
That had flown off the café nearby

It were a bit of good luck, that Connie had ducked
Managed to hang onto the battery on t'float
There were loads of blue sparks and they all fell apart
And landed in a thick cloud of smoke

Norm says "That's a relief, though I've lost half me teeth,
And me bike and me pole's all askew"
But the night-watchman bloke gave his brazier a poke
And made all his new pals a nice brew

It were later that day that poor Connie Gray
Explained to the Doc, best she could
"Flippin' lightnin'" she said "Just goes straight to me head"
"It's too much iron" he says "In yer blood"

She says "… Do you think, …it's the Guinness I drink?
I just have about six watchin' telly"
He says "Here's what we'll do, try to cut down to two,
And I'll get you some National Health wellies!"

Jacky The Night-Watchman's Dog

In the middle o' t'street by the Amblethwaite Arms
A hole stickin' up were reported
So the man from the Council had a look with 'is mate
And decided they'd best get it sorted

They put cones and red lights all around it
In case someone rode in on their bike
And they got a night-watchman to watch it
In case someone run off wi' it, like

I were on me way home one Wednesday night
And the bloke were sat all alone
So I stopped and we had a bit natter
And I noticed his dog with a bone

I were gettin' mesel' warm at the brazier
Cos we stood and we chatted a bit
His dog went in the hut and fetched out a stool
Blew the dust off and begged me to sit

"That's a right clever dog" I says to the bloke
But he just sat there shakin' 'is head
He says "Is he 'eck, he's a pain in the neck,
He's brung the stool with the wobbly leg"

Well I didn't mind that, so I give him a pat
And I sat there warmin' me toes
And the dog went ratchin' about in the hut
And come back wi' the bloke's dominoes

I says "Aah, ain't he canny, now what's he brought?"
And the dog laid the doms on a tray
Then he shuffled them round, picked up a hand
And nodded for us two to play

"Oh don't encourage him" the night-watchman says
"He's not as clever as what he makes out,
He thinks he's dead bright but he's not worth a light,
Just this mornin' I beat him three-nowt"

"You should see him play darts, he's hopeless,
He gets slavver all over the flights,
And he counts up by barkin', when he's doin' the markin',
He got us chucked out the pub Friday night"

Just then the dog gets a shovel of coal
And give the brazier a bit of a poke
Then he washed out some cups and poured out some tea
I says "He's clever" "He's not!" shouts the bloke

"He's been makin' my tea this last seven years,
You'd think he'd be getting' it right,
But I bet he's forgot and he's not warmed the pot,
I tell you, he's not worth a light"

So me and the dog had a few games of doms
I thought the way that the bloke talked were shockin'
But mind he were right the dog weren't much cop
Cos every other game he were knockin'

The bloke says "He likes poker, but acts like a joker,
The beggar just won't understand,
He can't help but fail, he keeps waggin' 'is tail,
Every time he gets dealt a good hand"

So the dog just went "Wuff" and sat in a huff
And picked up a novel instead
"Get away, you daft bat, don't know why you bought that,
You thought nowt of the film" the bloke said

So I had to say summat, he weren't bein' fair
I says "He looks pretty special to me"
He says "No, he's not right, he sometimes stops out all night,
And twice he's forgotten 'is key"

There's no pleasin' some folks, the grumpy old sod
A dog like that's not to be scoffed
That poor little lad, with him for a dad?
I just bid him goodnight and set off

Well the dog kept me company for part of the way
He says "It's allright. I'm needin' a walk,
I'll just see you down past the graveyard"
And I says "Flippin' heck! This dog talks!"

The dog stopped himself dead, slowly turnin' his head
And he stared in me eyes straight and true
He says "Don't say a word, don't tell HIM what you heard,
He'll have us answerin' the phone for him too"

Big Norm Gets Brought Down To Size

You know Big Norman Stokes? He's a pretty tough bloke
That's what most folks from Store Street are like
His only talent, it's said, were punchin' folks' heads
Well, that and mebbes ridin' a bike

Norm's a hard lad alright and quite fond of a fight
He's got one of them smacked-about faces
It's a right ugly mug, wi' two cauliflower lugs
An' a nose that's been broke in three places

His wife's a hairdresser, and 'is daughters are too
In fact, so's 'is neighbour an' all
"They're a right waste of space" he'd say, pullin' a face
"Even less use to someone who's bald"

"In fact there ain't no one here useful to me"
He were sayin' in Th'Amblethwaite Arms
"Yer all useless" he said, and sat shakin' 'is head
We said nowt 'case we come to some harm

"For instance, there's you" he were pointin' at Stu
Who works at the café in town
He says "What use are you?" He says "I make a nice brew"
"That's no use when me gutterin's come down"

"In't no one a builder?" he said quite bewildered
"Can't nobody do nowt to help?
If you weren't flamin' teachers or poets or preachers,
I'd not have to climb up meself"

"Don't know any builders" said the teacher's wife Hilda
"Exactly" says Norm "That's me point,
What's the use of a Bobby?" he says to young Robbie
"When me u-bend's got a leak at the joint"

Well Mr Carson the Parson were first to speak up
He says "I think Norm, you're bein' unfair,
There's folks here wi' talents" he said, bein' gallant
"But not quite what you're wantin' there"

"We've two dry-stone wallers and a bellrope installer,
A lollypop man and a porter,
There's a lamp post erector and a milestone inspector,
A shepherd an' a frozen-pea sorter"

"There's a jam-jar collector, a winkle prospector,
A rector, night-watchman, a sailor,
A hot air balloonist, an' a right good cartoonist,
A tanner, a judge, and a tailor"

"But I'm needin' a plumber, not some ceilidh-band drummer,
I want a brickie to sort out me wall,
I need me boiler put right, a new switch for t'big light,
And me roof needs some tiles on an' all"

As he looked round the bar "Good job I've no car"
He says "Cos you lot are not up to much,
If I needed t'mechanic, I'd be in a right panic,
There's no one could put right a clutch"

"Aye, right enough" said the milkman, Bill Clough
"Yer not wrong" says Librarian Lil
And the shepherd Will Scrote, just reached for 'is coat
And muttered "I'm away up the hill"

Well the room were all hushed as folks sat and blushed
Just how hopeless they felt you could tell
There were nobody spoke not even the bloke
In the raincoat who talked to himsel'

They just all sat and brooded "You're not included"
Says Norm to the barman Fred Wyatt
"You're functional, you are, stood there mindin' the bar,
Can you get us a pint while it's quiet?"

"And so what about me?" said Father Tralee
"Wasn't it me that Christened yer childer?"
"Who saw them over t'street?" said Lollipop Pete
"And taught them?" said the teacher's wife Hilda

Then the binman chipped in "Aye, who empty's yer bin?"
"Aye and who brings yer milk to yer door?"
Said the milkman Bill Clough who were feelin' quite tough
Cos he were sat with 'is mother-in-law

The chiropodist Jeff Gorman says "Anyway Norman,
What service might you be providing?
Could you fix a sore toe?" Norm says "Er, well no,
But I could give you a bloody good hiding"

When Harry Met Bella

Bella Blawhole, the big lass that lives down our backs
Were in the club Sat'day night watchin' telly
When in through the door walks this bloke, six foot four
And Bella felt her legs turn to jelly

She says "Wow! Over there" and Tessa says "Where?"
She says "Don't look –but just look at that lad"
She says "Where?" She says "There, that lad, but don't stare"
And Tessa says "Phwoar! He's not bad!"

She says "Aye, he's a smasher. I n'arf fancy him,
And look at the width of them shoulders,
Wouldn't mind a quick tussle wi' him and 'is muscles,
He's got pecs like a couple of boulders"

Now Bella's no oil paintin', it has to be said
And she's not all that good wi' the patter
It's cos o' this plight she's not found Mister Right
Mister Nearly-Right or Mister Wrong for that matter

110

So she jumped, poor lass, any chance that she got
Cos any bloke on his own were fair game
So she squeezed right up next to him, nonchalant like
And politely says "Hey, what's yer name?"

He says "Harry. What's yours?" She says "Bacardi and Coke,
And me mates there all drink Cherry-Bs"
He felt a right pratt, like, falling for that
But he coughed up and bought them all three

Then he ordered three Guinnesses just for himsel'
And he swallowed them down in one go
Bella says "Eeh, flippin heck" as they went down his neck
"There's no need to hurry you know"

But in one great big slurp then a sizable burp
The three pints were gone - just like that
Then he turned round to go but Bella says "Woah!
Are you not gonna stop for a chat?"

He says "No Love, I'm off. But I'll see you next year"
Bella says "Eh?" she says "How d'you mean?
I'm proper bamboozled, I'm used to refusals,
But this one's the quickest I've seen"

He says "It isn't you, Pet. So don't get upset,
But I'm not really a drinker you see,
It's just one night a year and that were it there,
Three pints and that's plenty for me"

"I'm one of triplets you see, there's two brothers and me,
And it's the three of our birthdays today,
It's a bugger because, you see, one lives in Oz,
And the other in the U S of A"

So wherever we are in the world on this day
We have a drink and we think for a while
And we think of each other, that's me and me brothers
It brings us dead close, sort of style

Having set Bella right he bid her goodnight
She were heartbroken and started to bawl
But her mates said "There there, he'll be back in a year"
Says Bella "I'll be waitin' an'all"

So the very next year she were sat sitting there
In the club. Mind, she waited for ages
She were dressed in her best, a new frock and clean vest
And a hairdo that cost a weeks wages

And like twelve month before, Harry walked through the door
And Bella felt her heart pitter-pound
Butterflies in her belly and her legs turned to jelly
As she jumped up to get in the round

Mind, he didn't look good, Bella thought, like he should
In fact there were a tear in his eye
His voice barely a whisper as he bent down and kissed her
She put her arm round him and he started to cry

'Stead o' three pints o' Guinness he only drank two
Bella thought "Poor lad's had a shock"
She started to wonder, mebbes the brother down-under
Had been swallowed by a dirty great croc

Mebbes Apaches had murdered the one in the States
Or he'd been shot by some gunslinger bloke
She says "Oh love, don't fret" but he were clearly upset
And his voice it were barely a croak

"I don't know what I've done to deserve this" he said
"Just once a year, wouldn't you think?
But as if just to spite us, I've gone and got laryngitis,
I'm on antibiotics – I can't drink!"

Uriah Uses His Loaf

Isaiah O'Dwyer 'ad a brother Uriah
He were twenty two stone, I dare say
There were no one surprised that he got to that size
Into bread, he were, in a big way

I don't mean inter-bred, I mean fond of a loaf
Din't mean Mum an' Dad were like cousins
Come to think of it though, you don't really know
Them O'Dwyers they breed by the dozen

It were nowt for Uriah to sit by 'is fire
Toastin' loaf after loaf after loaf
Wi' a big pot of butter, he behaved like a nutter
Which accounts for his abnormal growth

He were out of control, he'd eat buns, he'd eat rolls
French sticks till they come out his lugs
He loved crusty cobs which he'd pile in his gob
And drink tea, hot and sweet by the jug

Could be brown, could be white, even sliced were alright
Just as long as he'd plenty in stock
He indulged in baguettes but the strangest thing yet
'appened one day around four o'clock

Pushin' his barrow back down from the baker's in town
Past the park, when he saw t'baker's daughter
He'd to do double-take, she were stood by the lake
And were chuckin' good bread in the water

He says "Hey-ey-ey-ey! Are you chuckin' it away?"
She says "No, I'm just feedin' the ducks"
"Throwin' buns in to t'lake? You should be burnt at the stake!
That's perfectly good bread by the looks"

She says "No, it's me Dad's. It's just rejects he had,
You know, loaves that didn't turn out quite proper"
"That's a waste of good bread, you must be out o' yer head,
Stop that now, or I'm callin' the copper"

"But what about t'ducks?" …He says "Tough flippin' luck,
Kids starvin' in Africa, there are"
She says "Hold on a mo, I've a very good throw,
But I can't throw it that flippin' far!"

Uriah jumped in, nearly up to his chin
Shakin' ducks and tellin' em "Drop it!"
She continued to throw despite his shouts "No!"
He were expectin' by now she'd've stopped it

Then Uriah, he saw what he'd not seen before
She'd a sack-load of cobs goin' spare
And he thought, like you would "Why the hell am I stood,
In the water, with all that sat there?"

So he got himself out "Are you all right?" she shouts
He says "Aye! ...Is that lot buckshee?"
She says "It just gets chucked out. You can have it for nowt"
"Well in that case, I'm sorry" says he

"I don't mind if I do" he said, startin' to chew
On a multigrain twist what she had
A bit burnt at one end but he thought he'd make friends
And she too, thought Uriah weren't bad

So he invited her back, she'd to carry the sack
Cos Uriah were pushin' his barrow
She says "My name's Kate" and they got on just great
So Cupid couldn't miss with his arrow

He deduced, in all fairness, that a bakery heiress
Were likely to lead him astray
Summat electric had pass'd, between him and the lass
Not t'milk float it were too late in t'day

Uriah conspired to fulfil his desires
An' when she mentioned the two of 'em courting
He moved in like a shot, to her flat 'bove the shop
And indulged in quite serious cavortings

Cos when it shut for the day, they'd sneak down the back way
For a night of mad passionate lovin'
Interspersed wi' bein' fed wi' all manner of bread
Every time a fresh batch came out th'oven

When she showed him her baps, he nearly collapsed
Cos most folk had only heard rumours
They were better by far than those baked by her Pa
And were almost the size of her bloomers

Now Uriah and Kate have enough on their plate
Ignoring all the gossip, you know
But tongues wag away, and it's true what they say
He married her just for her dough

Ruby Ruddick's Bad Luck

It were the day of the races, The Amblethwaite Plate
Ruby Ruddick were tryin' on her hat
When her budgerigar, shouted "Go away, Ma!"
Only he said it a bit ruder than that!

She didn't bat an eye, she just simply let fly
With her slipper which bounced of 'is cage
Joey swung on 'is perch as 'is cage sort o' lurched
He shouts "Hey, you daft gowk, act yer age"

His door got flung open so he went for a fly
And Ruby just heard a wet splat
He'd relieved himself right down the front of her frock
Then he pecked a great chunk from her hat

She spilt her tea down her lap and tripped over the cat
And laddered her best pair of tights
She says "Ooh, that's a pain, I'll have to get dressed again"
But she were used to things not going right

She were never the luckiest of folks weren't poor Rube
But she'd no time for tantrums or sobs
She put rouge on her cheeks, a bit talc on her nose
And got a Murraymint to put in her gob

She left home and set off along Bolsover Street
And she tried not to step on the cracks
Or walk under ladders or step on folks' shadders
Or follow in anyone's tracks

She got t'wrong tram to t'races and had to get off
And take a shortcut through Amblethwaite woods
But it took twice as long and she were starting to pong
Cos o' some stinky stuff in which she'd just stood

On the other side o' t'canal she saw Doris, her pal
But she couldn't see a bridge anywhere
She shouts "How do I get to the other side, pet?"
And Doris shouts "Yer already there!"

There were three races left when she got to the track
With her hair in a mess and all mucky
But she decided she'd still have a flutter cos, hey
One of these days she'd get lucky

She had a look at the horses in the paddock out back
And she made up her mind then and there
Cos she saw Father Tralee from St Wilfreds R.C.
Blessing this big chestnut mare

She thought that's just the job as she took out ten bob
And she whispered a "Thank-you" to Heaven
And to Slick Sid the bookie, she says "I'm feeling right lucky,
I'll have ten bob to win – number seven"

Well it won by a mile and our Rube were all smiles
As she picked up her winnings and then
Thought she might go and see if Father Tralee
Were doing the business again

So back round the paddock, she looked over the rail
There were piebalds and skewbalds and bays
And she spotted him stood, to his ankles in mud
Saying a prayer to this big dappled-grey

She went straight to Slick Sid and put on seven quid
He says "I hope your good luck's not contagious"
It romped home in first place. What a picture, Sid's face
As he paid Ruby a good two months' wages

She were excited as the runners for the last race come out
And she kept an eye out for the lucky old Priest
And there right enough, he were doin' his stuff
This time blessing quite a sad looking beast

But she were straight to the bookie, put everything on
Even her catalogue cash, two pound ten
Slick Sid rubbed 'is hands, he thought "Hey, this is grand,
Never thought I'd see that lot again"

Then - they're off! Round the course at a hell of a lick
But Ruby's horse started to stumble and totter
Half way down the stand side it just lay down and died
As dead as a pickled pig's trotter

Ruby ran to the jockey, grabbed his throat with both hands
Saying "Hey, what's goin on? What's the score?"
The jockey scratched 'is head an' looked puzzled and said
"The beggar's never done that before"

"Just my luck" Ruby thought and had to resort
To Shanks's pony for the four mile walk home
And she'd done about three when she saw Father Tralee
Ruby thought she might just pick-a-bone

She says "Lose your shirt, pet?" He says "Me? I don't bet"
"Stop fibbin', I saw you" she said
"I'd a bet on those two - but your third din't come through,
That one in the last that dropped dead"

Poor Father Tralee, he says "Oh, Deary me"
He says "You're not one of us Catholics, then?"
She says "No" He says "Oh" She says "How do you know?"
He says "Listen, I'll give you the gen"

"It's like this, you see, you've barked up the wrong tree,
In my job you do see some sights,
But if you'd stood near you'd've heard loud and clear,
I was giving t'poor beggar the last rites"

Stan Brown Is So Cool!

Stan Brown, last back-end, got driven round t'bend
In cold weather he wished he weren't born
No way were he ever gonna score wi' the girls
Not dressed up to the nines to keep warm

He were always a cold one, were Stanley, poor lad
Fire right up the chimney most days
With 'is chair pulled up close just toastin' 'is toes
And a rug on 'is knees just in case

He hated Thursdays in winter it were shoppin' day see
He'd get dragged down town, like it or not
He'd have to stand in the queues until he turned blue
For the few measly bits that they got

He put on three pairs of socks made of thick Shetland wool
And he pulled them right up to 'is knees
And a few laggy bands to like keep them up there
But they still didn't keep out the breeze

Now the Army-and-Navy's 'is favourite shop
He went there the week afore last
He got a hat that's designed for the Arctic Patrol
But it still didn't keep out the blast

He got triple lined, thick fleecy boots for to wear
They were meant for a trip to the Pole
He got two sizes too big to fit over 'is socks
But they still didn't keep out the cold

He had thermal long-johns that he'd got off 'is Dad
From 'is armpits right down to the socks
Then he thought he'd best wear them two pairs at a time
Cos 'is knees just refused not to knock

He got sheepskin lined earmuffs and double-glazed specs
And a muffler pulled up round 'is nose
He ate hot vindaloos made wi' Fisherman's Friends
But it still didn't warm up 'is toes

Now the lad in the shop says "I've just what you need,
To keep out the wind when it's parky,
They're quilted legwarmers from the Russian Frontier,
In a nice shade of camouflaged khaki"

So he put a pair on then he needed some pants
To fit over t'top o' the lot
So he dug out some ski pants that were two inches thick
But they still didn't keep him that hot

With two, double-knit vests and a lumberjack shirt
And a waistcoat of cavalry twill
He looked in the mirror and said "Just the job"
But it still didn't keep out the chill

He says "Give us a jumper like the sailors all wear,
And I don't give a damn what it costs"
So he put a one on, it came down to 'is knees
But it still didn't keep out the frost

Now the Swiss Border Patrol do a nice fur-lined parka
With a hood aimed to keep out the snow
But with all the zips fastened, 'is nose still stuck out
And the bugger just started to glow

When 'is fingers got cold he were startin' to think
He were nearin' the end of 'is wits
He got thick woolly liners for some motorbike gloves
And a big pair of sheepskin lined mitts

But when he went out it had started to rain
He'd a brolly to keep off the splatter
But with 'is hand out 'is pocket to hold it aloft
Well 'is teeth they just started to chatter

I saw him in th'Amblethwaite Arms Friday night
His big snow boots and hood up an'all
And 'is dirty great mitts, he found it quite hard to sit
So he stood next to t'fire on t'far wall

He looked owt but manly "There's a rum for you Stanley"
Said the barmaid whose name were Big Eve
He were willin' to pay'er but he'd so many layers
His money were quite hard to retrieve

He says "You know, I've just thought, instead of a rum,
I think I'll have a bottle of beer,
Straight off the cold shelf wi' some ice cubes chucked in,
Is it me or is it quite hot in here?"

The Night Dan Joblin Proposed

When Dan Joblin turned ninety on August the third
His drinkin' pals passed round the hat
They collected enough for a bit of a do
For Big Bella the kissogram, n'that

Cos as well as our Dan bein' the Kleeneze Man
He was also part time Concert Chairman
He booked the turns at the Amblethwaite Excelsior Club
Havin' retired from bein' a poss-tub repairman

He were well known and well liked in Amblethwaite, Dan
So the place were full up for 'is do
All 'is friends from the Club and the lads from the Pub
And the Volunteer Fire Brigade crew

It was at times like this he'd get a tear in 'is eye
Cos he wished his wife Marge were still with 'im
She'd eloped wi' Tom Turnbull while Dan had 'is hands full
Wi' the charabanc trip out to Lytham

So he missed havin' a female companion
Thinkin' he's far too old for the lasses
His heart wasn't in it, he didn't know why
Even 'is hormones, he felt, needed glasses

His first love had been Marge with her pearly white teeth
Unto whom he'd been true ever since
A brunette wi' blue eyes, but at his time of life
He'd settle for cataracts, no teeth and blue rinse

Well, old Mavis Penrose just fitted the bill
And she were sat there just turned eighty-nine
Tappin' her feet to Dodgy Ray on the organ
Accompanied on drums by Sid Grimes

Dan waited while they played summat slower
An' got her up for the Saint Bernard's Waltz
Thinkin' "Eh up, I've scored" as they danced round the floor
You'd never guess that 'is left leg were false

That's right, he'd lost it in t'Second World War
He's never let it bother him, though
Just afore crossin' the Rhine, he'd stepped on a mine
Blew his leg off ….right down to 'is toe.

When they played summat fast, Mavis thought she should ask
She says "You game?" He says "Aye, okey-dokey"
And they bopped like two kids, then stayed up and did
The Gay Gordons and the old Hokey-cokey

Then they sat down exhausted and finished their drinks
And took a minute or two to unwind
"Hey, Mavis?" says Dan, as he reached for her hand
"I'll walk you home. Er, that's if you don't mind"

There were no moon that night, it were black as Marmite
They crossed the road just beside t'Jubilee
Then he had an idea, - I blame the beer
And he turned and went down on one knee

She thought 'is leg'd come out "Whassamatter?" she shouts
Grabbin' hold of him by 'is lapels
It were too dark to see he were down on one knee
He says "I'm all right don't worry yersel"

He says "Mavis, my love, my sweet turtle-dove,
You're makin' me heart all a flutter"
Then he blurted it out "D'you wanna get married or owt?"
And poor Mavis just stood there and stuttered

"Mer-mer-married?" she said "Yer per-per-pullin me leg,
I'd love to!" and she stifled her blushes
He says "I know I'm just Dan, the Kleeneze man,
But you'd never want for mop-heads or brushes"

Dan kissed her goodnight and skipped all the way home
He felt like he'd just been reborn
And that night he dreamt of the evenin' he'd spent
But he'd a problem when he woke the next morn

You see, when you get older and things start to go
And your memory's well, not at its best
Dan knew he'd proposed to Mavis Penrose
But couldn't remember if she'd said 'Yes'

128

So he went to the box at the end of their street
And dialled Amblethwaite one-three-five-two
His leg went all weak when he heard Mavis speak
"It's Dan Joblin" he says "Is that you?"

He says "Remember last night, I went down on one knee,
Just next to the Jubilee wall,
And I asked you to marry us, - did you say yes?
Cos I'm buggered if I can recall"

She says "Oh, it's you, Dan - I'm so pleased you rang,
Cos me problem is sorted at last,
You see, I know I said YES! But I have to confess,
I've been sittin' here wonderin' who'd asked!"

Isaiah O'Dwyer Retires

Isaiah O'Dwyer were asleep by the fire
When the Parson called round for a drink
"I were havin' a nap" he'd 'is bible on t'lap
"I should be swottin' for t'finals d'you think?"

When you've turned ninety two, there's not much left to do
Once Meals-on-Wheels and t'library van's been
He were bored were Isaiah, he'd set 'is sights higher
But not achieved, if you know what I mean

Now Mr Carson the Parson from St Bob's C of E
Helped himself to a whisky from t'shelf
A ritual he'd observed for forty odd years
Although Isaiah never touched it himself

He says "Now then, Isaiah. I haven't seen you at choir,
Two months now, you've not sung a note"
He looked sad did Isaiah, "I'm gonna have to retire"
He said wi' a lump in 'is throat

"Retire, Isaiah? Yer life's love were that choir,
I mean, I know that you don't sing in key,
You've no voice poor soul, you couldn't shout 'Coal'
But that's just between you and me"

He were wise, were Isaiah, he knew he were dire
And in hopes that he might not get heard
He'd got right good at mimin' and you'd think by the timin'
Of 'is lips he were singin' each word

"I'm gettin' old" says Isaiah "I'm easily tired,
I'm destined to sit here alone,
It's such a long trek, me bad leg, me bad neck,
It's time I were put in a home"

The Parson says "Ooh," he says "That's not like you,
I'm gonna get Doctor on t'phone"
The Doc came straight away, and the Parson had stayed
Cos he din't like to leave him alone

"Turn your head to the window, and stick out your tongue,
- - Now waggle it" said Doctor McSweet.
"Do I have to?" He says "Aye" Isaiah says "Why?"
"Cos I don't like that bloke over t'street"

He says "Yer bad legs got worse. Best see t'District Nurse,
It's old age is that, Mr O'Dwyer'
If you're ninety two, then this leg 'ere is too"
"But t'other's same age" said Isaiah

The next day Mrs Phelps, that's Isaiah's Home-help
Suggested a move to Fellview
A retirement home where folks end up goin'
When they've not got much else left to do

"You'll love it in there, you don't have to climb stairs,
There's bingo and sing-songs and stuff,
They've got dominoes and cards, mini-golf in the yard"
But Isaiah just sat not too chuffed

He thought it over for weeks then gave in, so to speak
Thought he'd better get shot of some kit
He put an advert in t'paper, The Amblethwaite Post
'For sale, gent's grey suit, perfect fit'

So it came the big day, he were sad in a way
Cos he'd lived 'is whole life number three
Old Suggett and Son the removal men come
His empty house were a sad sight to see

He were findin' it hard. He'd a last look round t'yard
And the memories flowed back with the tears
His initials in t'gate, carved when he were eight
And the back wall where he'd played mountaineers

There were the nail where the tin bath had hung on the wall
And the slate for the knocker-up man
The clothesline, long gone, where 'is father's long-johns
Were hung out every Monday by Mam

He got into the van with 'is suitcase in hand
When the loadin' and that were complete
Mrs Phelps waved goodbye with a tear in her eye
As the van pulled away down the street

He got to Fellview and they helped him on out
Straightaway like he knew he belonged
He turned round and he gave Mrs Phelps a big wave
Cos Fellview? It's just four doors along!

The Amblethwaite Secret Allotment Society

A penny-pinchin' bloke were big Norman Stokes
If he'd measles, wouldn't give yer a spot
More chance of a drink from a Mormon I'd think
Born wi' cramp in 'is fist, like as not

In fact all of them folk from th'allotment pulled strokes
To avoid them from partin' wi stuff
That they'd go there and grow, all year round, row by row
You'd think they'd have more than enough

But Norm were a funny un, wouldn't part wi' an onion
Not a turnip or cauli to spare
The hours he'd spend, you'd think, for a friend
The odd leek, once a week, would be fair?

But no, you got nowt, not one measly sprout
Not just Norm mind, there's three or four others
Night and day, so they say, up there, plantin' away
But not even a tater for mother

Now you know that I'm not one for tellin' of tales
It were Big Hec that first smelt a rat
In the pub Friday night he said "Just isn't right,
Our neighbours bein' stingy like that"

It were then that the grocer, Miss Trevithick sat closer
(Too many teeth for one gob!)
But nice enough though, and she says "Do you know?
There's summat quite strange 'bout that mob"

I forget what she said, it went straight out me head
Her teeth put us off, to be blunt
Like a mouthful of boulders, stood shoulder to shoulder
An' queuin' up to get to the front

But she reckoned, that lot, bought their veg at her shop
"Buy their veg?" says Stan Brown "Flippin' 'eck"
"So they don't grow their own?" says Young Nobby Bowen
"There's a rabbit off there" says Big Hec

"What I think we should do" Hector says, "Me and you,
And Nobby, when no one's about,
Just to see what occurs, of what we're not aware,
We should sneak in and check the place out

But the wall were right tall an' a thick un an'all
It's part of the old monastry's doin's
Henry th'Eighth and 'is bods, in fifteen hundred an' odd
Had come up an' they'd left it in ruins

"No problem" said Hec, loosenin' 'is neck
"I've a telegraph pole on me truck,
I'm an expert, I am, wi' a batterin' ram"
Which, as it 'appened, were a right stroke o' luck

There's a dirty great door about ten foot by four
In t'front wall but it weren't any match
For Big Hec and 'is ram, it were money for jam
As the door an' its frame were dispatched

Now we hadn't intended to be apprehended
Cos that were us little plan spoiled
I nearly dropped dead. A commotion in t'shed,
And Big Norm, he bust out like a boil

See, Big Norman Stokes ain't the nicest of blokes
He'd frighten a dog off its bone
And though allotments, by rights, should be quiet at nights
He were there …an' he weren't on 'is own

Cos out come Tim Jones, Will Scrote and Tom Bowen
Bert McGarr, Dodgy Ray and Bill Clough
They were all worse for wear, they'd been drinkin' in there
And all looked decidedly rough

I thought we'd get battered but it didn't seem to matter
Cos from the shed came a gurglin' type roar
They saw me, Hec and Nobby and not Robbie the Bobby
They said "Get in quick and shut t'flamin door!"

Now me, Hec and Nobby are in on the hobby
As long as we don't spill the beans
Turnip vodka's the reason we're there in all seasons
Puttin' th' hours in, if you know what I mean

More'n an acre in there, wi' not one inch to spare
There's turnips and not a thing but
There's a turnip-mash mill an' a shed full of stills
And up top there's a bottlin' hut

Since they got a bit edgy, once a week, they buy veggies
At the market 'bout ten miles away
It's money well spent, just to put folks off t'scent
A stone o'carrots really goes a long way

There's a meetin' o' t'committee on Fridays, it's a pity
That there aren't no more members we need
But I'll put yer name down, cos if word gets around
I don't think we could cope wi' t'stampede

Wilfy Spode Looks For Summat To Eat

Old Wilfy Spode were a gent of the road
A traveller, a tramp you might say
He lived on his wits and fed on the bits
Of food that the rich chuck away

He'd always been poor since the day he were born
His family never had t'wherewithal
He can see his dad yet, sat out on t'back step
And wishing they'd a house like, an'all

Ma fed them throughout. She'd make a meal out of nowt
She'd feed a family of four wi' one moth
Or she'd strip out the bones from her corsets
And boil up a nice pan of broth

So he grew to be nifty at poachin' did Wilf
And were partial to the odd bit o' grouse
Which meant that he weren't very popular
Wi' the Squire, …him that lived at big house

There were one day last May he was down t'Squire's way
And were washing his feet in the pond
And by a sheer stroke of luck, along comes a duck
And of roast duck, our Wilf, were quite fond

He remembered he still had a bit of stale bread
Which he used to entice the duck near
Then he grabbed it by t'throat, shoved it straight in 'is coat
Making sure that the coast were still clear

It were a couple of days since Wilf had been fed
So he started a fire then and there
And he sat down wi' t'duck and he started to pluck
And the duck, you could tell, were quite scared

Just then the Gamekeeper appeared at the top of the field
Wilf got in a bit of a flap
He threw t'duck back in t'pond, like where it belonged
And pretended he were havin' a nap

But the Gamey had spotted the duck splashin' round
And the feathers. He says "Hey what are those?"
And Wilf says "It's him. He's just gone for a swim,
And I'm sittin' here mindin' his clothes"

So our Wilf got escorted from off the Squire's land
With a number nine boot up his rump
It were getting near dark so he went to the park
But found his favourite bench were gazumped

It were old Herby Scrote who were in the same boat
But were missin' a couple of screws
He says the "Last time I saw you, you didn't turn up!"
Wilf says "I know, I were down wi' the flu"

"I'm starving" says Wilf "Have you got owt to eat?"
Old Herby says "No, I've been fed,
I've just had mince n'dumplins at Mrs McSomething's"
"How the hell d'you cop that, then?" Wilf said

"You just pick up a nice crusty old cowpat,
And knock on the first door you see,
Dead easy" he said "You just ask for some bread,
To make your own sandwich for tea"

"They take one look at t'pat an' say *'You're not eating that,
Come in and have summat wi' us'*,
It works every time, they invite you to dine,
And it ends up they make a right fuss"

"You'll have to give it a try" So Wilf says "Well, aye,
I might go'n try that farm up the top,
Hungry as a cow in a car park, I am,
I could murder a nice big pork chop"

So he set off up t'lane then across the front field
Picked a crusty old cowpat on t'way
And when t'bloke come to t'door, Wilf were starin' at t'floor
Tuggin' a forelock, he started to say...

He says "Sorry to trouble you, but I'm down on me luck,
Could you spare us two slices of bread?
I've got me own cowpat, some nettles, n'that,
I can make me own sandwich" he said

The bloke said to poor Wilf "You can't eat that filth!"
Mind, he'd heard about Wilf and his schemin'
He says "I'll fetch some bread, have a look in t'cow-shed,
There'll be fresh'uns in there that's still steamin'"

A Monumental Cock-up

Honest, God fearin' folks were the Tuckers
With a cravin' for saintly protection
Dulcie handed out hymn-books on Sundays
And Sid handed round the collection

They'd invested in t'plot when Sid first retired
"It won't come in wrong" Dulcie said
"We'll order a headstone wi' cherubs and doves,
To celebrate the lives we have led"

The celebration came quicker than Dulcie had planned
It came as a shock to poor Sid
She'd just popped into town for their pensions
When the grim reaper did what he did

They were layin' new tarmac on t'High Street
With diggers and rollers and that
She stepped out from behind Hec Schole's wagon
And got rolled out herself, nice and flat

Now with all the arrangements that Sid had to make,
He were pleased that they'd sorted the stone
All he needed now were the epitaph inscribed
So he got Chippy Scott on the phone

Now, Chippy Scott, the Monumental Mason
Took the epitaph down line by line
It were a right fittin' verse Sid had chosen
And it ended wi' 'GOD SHE WERE THINE'

Chippy said "Aye Sid, I don't see a problem,
It'll just take a couple of days,
I've taken a lad on this mornin',
I'll get him on wi' it, more or less, straight away"

The next couple of days were long ones for Sid
Gettin' used to him bein' alone
So he took the dog for a walk up the graveyard
To have a quick look at the stone

He struck a match so's to see the inscription
Took a swig from 'is hip flask o' gin
It were a right fittin' verse Sid had chosen
But it ended wi' 'GOD SHE WERE THIN'

He were on t'phone to Chippy next mornin' at eight
Says "You know this 'GOD SHE WERE THINE' ?
Well your young apprentice has cocked it all up,
He's missed the 'E' off the last bloody line"

When you consider the nature of poor Dulcie's death
He couldn't apologise more
He says "I'll send him back up to re-do it,
As soon as he walks through that door"

Now the service were nice, not a long one
It were wet but there were still a few there
With heads bowed in sorrow at the graveside
They solemnly gathered in prayer

Sid's tear-filled eyes strayed to the headstone
And thoughts of just what might've been
It were a right fittin' verse Sid had chosen
But now it ended 'EEEh, GOD SHE WERE THIN!'

A Bridge Too Full

You'll not remember that derby-match, year afore last
It's washed from all decent folks minds
Plodgeborough come down to play Amblethwaite Town
Just the thought sends a shiver down t'spine

Not a Cup -Final, you know, nowt as trivial as that
The thought of losin' to THEM were absurd
We don't really mention them Plodgers by name
Here in Amblethwaite it's like a rude word

Now me uncle, John Platt, weren't into all that
He were t'sort who'd sooner watch cricket
But 'is Dad had just died, so wi' true Amblethwaite pride
He decided he'd not waste the ticket

So he got himself dressed in 'is Dad's stripey vest
Lucky undies, full o' holes, dirty grey
Lucky trousers that had witnessed the top of the league
So had obviously seen better days

Now the rain it had poured on the Amblethwaite hordes
From mid-mornin' till late afternoon
But their spirits were high as they tucked into t'pies
Even though it were like a monsoon

It were previous back-end, the roof blew off the stand
So that made the rain ten times worse
It dripped off John's cap an' it ran down 'is back
While 'is shoes and 'is socks got immersed

But 'is Dad would be proud seein' John in the crowd
And joinin' in t'songs wi' the rest
He pulled 'is coat over 'is head "Hey up" someone said
"That blokes got a blue and white vest"

He hadn't a clue, stood in Amblethwaite blue
While the rest were in Plodgeborough red
Must've got in a muddle whilst watchin' the puddles
And gone in at their end instead

"There's an Ambler down there! shouts a bloke wi' long hair
And they caught the poor lad by surprise
As twenty big Plodgers all jumped on poor John
And he dropped four or five of 'is pies

Well, he did best he could as they prodded and shoved
But the fight it spilled out on to t'pitch
As the winger MacFaul, wrapped 'is foot round the ball
An' it hit John on t'side of 'is snitch

Now it were purely a fluke, cos John hadn't looked
As the ball bounced off side of 'is nose
But, even worse yet, into Amblethwaite's net
Just as t'Ref brought the game to a close

So the Plodgers all cheered while the Amblers like jeered
Then hung their heads low wi' the shame
Of bein' beaten by arch rivals Plodgeborough
By a nose, right at end o' the game

There were folk everywhere in the depths of despair
In tears as they thought of their team
Gettin' beaten one-nowt, they just felt clapped out
They'd nowt left to live for, it seemed

Then the tears turned to sneers and some serious leers
As attention it turned to our John
Poor lad were disgraced, wouldn't dare show 'is face
In the Amblethwaite Arms from then on

Now old Dodger the Plodger were on 'is way home
He were crossin' the Plodgeborough Bridge
When he noticed a lad in a blue and white vest
Standin' a bit close to the edge

He thought it looked queer and when he got nearer
There's our John gettin' ready for Jumpin'
He shouts "Hey lad, there's no need to go over the top,
Just cos your team got a bloody good thumpin"

"Anyway, don't chuck yoursel' off Plodgeborough's bridge,
You've got one back home you could use"
John held back a tear and says "I couldn't get near,
You should see t'flippin' length of the queues!"

Amblethwaite Revisited

An old flyin' saucer from the planet Beebop
Were hoverin' low in the sky
The aliens inside were sick of their lives
If you're bothered I'll tell you for why

It were on account of this mission, they'd been on it for years
The poor lads weren't havin' much luck
Their computer were down, their radar were out
And the door to the bathroom were stuck

They were cold they were hungry, half rations of food
They had no clean clothes to put on
They din't know where they were, their headlights were bust
The demister and wipers were gone

Then one of them, Zogg, has this brilliant idea
He says "I'll see if I can feel where we are"
He said "I'll stick me hand through that hole in the floor"
The Captain says "Hey, you're a star"

So they came down right low, as low as they dared
And Zogg put 'is hand through the gap
His mates got excited and gathered around
Sayin' "What a courageous young chap"

He says "Hang on a bit, I've got summat here"
"What is it then, Zogg?" says young Blork
"I think it's the Statue of Liberty,
We must be hoverin' over New York"

"We're miles off our course" the Captain declared
We're not even in the right land
So they zoomed away up as Zogg got to 'is feet
And started to thaw out 'is hand

It were a couple of days before they tried it again
And the Captain brought the craft right down low
He shouted for Zogg, he says "Come do your stuff"
Zogg says "Allright then, I'll give it a go"

He squeezed 'is hand through the gap and had a bit grope
The others all stood around helpless
Then he felt summat metal that were stickin' up high
"It's the Eiffel Tower" he says "We're in Paris"

The Captain says "Great, were not far away now,
We'll soon get this thing back on track"
He says to young Zogg "You're doin' a grand job,
You'll get a medal If wuz ever get back"

A few hours had passed when the craft swooped back down
And young Zogg put 'is hand through the hole
He groped and he groped but he couldn't find owt
And 'is fingers were numb, poor soul

He kept feelin' for landmarks and bits that stuck up
And they plotted their course every hour
Like the Bridge over t'Forth and the Angel o' t'North
But he still never found Blackpool Tower

Then they hovered over Amblethwaite Cokeworks
He burnt 'is fingers on the flame from the top
He gave the crew a right fright when he jumped up a height
But he shouted for the driver to stop

Then he shouts "Hold it there, I can feel summat weird,
It feels a bit strange and hotch potch"
It's Amblethwaite, oh hell" They said "How can you tell?"
He says "Cos some beggar's just nicked me watch"

Uncle Bobby's One-Ton Pigeon

Down behind the allotments where Norm keeps 'is hens
There's a cree, like you've not seen afore
It's fifty yards wide, armour plated outside
And wi' cast iron shutters for t'doors

It's where Bob keeps his pigeon. He's just got the one
Sits on scaffold wi' a skip for 'is bait
It's an ostrich been crossed wi' a Clydesdale, folks say
Eats pies and drinks beer by the crate

Now his very first race, there weren't enough space
To load him on t'van wi' the rest
They phoned Pickfords Removals for a pan-techno-thing
And when he saw it, well, t'bird got distressed

151

They fastened on 'is harness and pushed and they shoved
They levered and hammered and cursed
And after an hour of blood, sweat and tears
They loaded him in, …back-end first

He pecked a hole in t'back shutters so's to see t'goings on
And a teardrop sorta dripped from his beak
Cos he'd never been away since he'd first come to stay
Well not very far so to speak

Then me poor Auntie Winnie sobbed into her pinny
And begged them, sayin' "Please let him stay"
But brave Uncle Bob just says "Oh, shut yer gob,
He'll be back in a couple o' days"

Then the wagon set out on its long journey south
Cos the start of the race were in Wales
With its head stickin' out, poor bugger knew nowt
While Uncle Bobby sat bitin' his nails

Now when they got down there wi' all t'other birds
As soon as he felt the van stop
He bust through the shutters and had a bit flutter
Saying "I've had enough, lads. I'm off"

Well all t'other pigeons got scattered around
A poor copper got blown off his bike
As he circled around till 'is bearings he found
And dropped stuff to show his dislike

Folks dived for cover as he soared 'bove their heads
Left a path like a flamin' typhoon
Old ladies picked poodles up or hid under beds
When they heard him let off t'sonic boom

Within minutes he were high over Liverpool town
The Air-Traffic bloke says "Ey, Hang about!
What's at ten thousand feet?" He went white as a sheet
"Phone the Raf!" he shouts "They'll sort it out"

He were fast, were the pigeon, there's no doubtin' that
But his pace were like inconsequential
It's not speed you need if you want to succeed
Knowin' where you live, like, is just as essential

Well the bird were quite thirsty and when he spied Lakes
He dived down just to have a quick whet
But he made such a splash that the hills were awash
An' Bolton's water supply under threat

Back and forth across t'Pennines wi' revitalised zest
He showed up on the radars once more
Two Tornado jets buzzed him but couldn't keep up
And they still don't believe what they saw

When they made their report, they said "It was sort,
Of a great pigeon shaped U.F.O."
That had flown overhead just this side o' Nenthead
"Well get after it!" shouts their C.O.

But by now he'd picked up on the Amblethwaite scent
It were a gasworks and boneyard type smell
It were still fifty mile but he started to smile
Cos there were a slight whiff of steak pie as well

He left the jets standin', got home in a flash
There's still a gouge twenty foot wide
Where he landed on t'field, turned head over heels
An' did a hundred and fifty yard slide

It were five minutes later the jets flew on past
The two pilots radioed to base
"Yon U-F-O's lost!" they said to their boss
"Must've gone up a height into space"

Little did they know, when they gave up on t'search
The pigeon were safe in his cree
With a half-dozen pails of the very best ale
And a skipload of pies for his tea

And still round his neck, like a trophy were hung
A memento to which he'd earned t'right
It were a set of blue shutters that shook when he fluttered
And said 'Pickfords Removals' in white

Jack Peake Gets What's Coming

When Amblethwaite Wanderers got knocked out the league
By the B-team from Beswick-on-Sea
I said "Oh to pot! Had enough! That's yer lot,
When I were bad they didn't come to see me"

It were a game of two halves and both of 'em bad
You talk about mountains to climb?
No kidding, they couldn't kick their own backsides
I saw a parrot throwin' up at half time

Not all games were bad - some were cancelled
I blame big Jack Peake - that's the boss
He sold all our best blokes. Was he having a joke?
It seemed like he din't give a toss

He were as much use as sleeves in a trilby, were Jack
Not the sort of bloke you could trust
He took the team on a daytrip to Blackpool
Just to get a ride on an open-top bus

They dropped down a division every year, last three years
Till there weren't any left, so to speak
Not unless you count playing on Sundays in t'park.
Against pot-bellied old blokes past-their-peak

See the atmosphere's gone since the crowd dropped right off
It once were a wonderful sight
But I felt daft on me own stood there singing
And I'd to walk fifty yards for a light!

Anyway Jack got the sack not long after that
And he left without makin' a fuss
He found his car had been nicked so he felt double sick
Cos he'd to walk into town for the bus

He hadn't got further than the top of the street
He saw this wife having a bit of a bubble
"Help us out mate, me money's rolled down the grate,
If I don't get me man's chips there'll be trouble"

He were normally dead tight but he said "Oh, allright"
And reluctantly give her ten bob
An' though she knew he were Jack Peake and a bit of a geek
She smacked a great sloppy kiss on his gob

"That were worth it were that" he said, straightenin' his hat
And blushin' wi a smile - ear t' ear
Then he saw this poor tramp holding out a tin cup
He says "Don't worry old lad, - have this here"

So he give him ten bob, t'lad says "Cor, just the job,
I'll get the wife and the bairns a bit tea"
Jack says "No, here look, there's another for luck"
He says "Have a coupla' fish suppers – on me!"

It made him feel good being kind, like you should
And he stuck out his chest like dead chuffed
Then he realised that he'd just spent his bus fare
So his chest went back in like - dead huffed

He took a shortcut 'cross Amblethwaite marshallin' yards
And it started to persistently rain
He inadvertently stepped on the mainline
And got flattened by the Doncaster train

So he turns up at heaven, St Peter's stood there
Says "Bugger me, if it isn't Jack Peake!
You needn't've bothered, you're not welcome here,
I think you've a right flaming cheek"

Jack says "Give us a chance, I've had a right awful day,
I've been sacked, robbed and soaked in the rain,
I gave me last thirty bob to some needier folks,
And then you had us knocked down by a train"

St Peter says "Aye, well you get days like that,
You should try working here it's a pain,
Stood standin' all day wi yer feet in a cloud,
Does nowt for your varicose veins"

He says "Go sling yer hook and he slammed closed the book,
You're not getting' in here, there's no way,
It's too late turning nicey, all sugar and spicy,
In the last hour of your last flamin' day"

Jack were stuck what to do, he were holding up t'queue
"Where'll I go then I cannot go back?"
"Somewhere hot, like as not -I don't give a jot,
There's some brochures over there in that rack"

"You're s'posed to forgive us me sins and let us come in"
Says Jack, his pulse startin' to quicken
"Go an' have a word wi' God, he'll give us the nod"
Peter says "Right, but don't count any chickens"

It were nobbut two minutes, Saint Peter comes back
"I've a message to you from the boss"
He says "Here y'are Jack, here's yer thirty-bob back,
Now think yerself lucky –Get lost!"

O Little Town Of Amblethwaite

There's a shop right nextdoor to the Amblethwaite Zoo
That's owned by the sisters Trevithick
The sign 'bove the door just says 'General Store'
'Spose that's cos it sells nowt specific

I were in there one day buying upside-down nails
For fixing the ceiling in t'lobby
I were stood in the queue looking round like you do
When in walks young Robbie, the Bobby

"'Ello, 'ello, 'ello. What's going on here?"
He addressed all us folks there assembled
And even though I were totally innocent like
I suddenly felt guilty and trembled

He says "Acting on information received from me box,
At the corner o'canal path and t'cut,
I mounted me bicycle and proceeded here quick,
Cos I've heard there's strange doin's afoot"

"There's someone illegal that's alienating here,
So I'm sure that you'll all understand,
That I'll have to search t'premises, bottom to top,
And investigate owt underhand"

It were then that he noticed crouched down behind t'till
Summat that din't quite look law-abiding
It were a dirty great polar bear eleven foot tall
With 'is head in a carrier bag, hidin'

Miss Trevithick says "Oh" like nowt were amiss
"Oh, him? That's er, Snowy, me dog,
You can't be too careful, wi break-ins and such"
And the Bobby just stood there agog

He says "That there's the illegal alien, is that!"
"An Alien?" she says "Don't be daft,
Aliens are green wi' ten eyes and six lugs"
And at that all us punters just laughed

Well Robbie the Bobby got quite angry at that
And he scowled as he reached for his book
Then lickin' his pencil he started to write
As poor Snowy just stood there and shook

He came out from behind and just looked at his feet
Said "It's a fair cop, Guv. I don't want no trouble"
And the Bobby reached up and grabbed hold of his scruff
And he were marched down to t'station at t'double

Now the Sergeant asked a right load of questions
As for mitigation poor Snowy appealed
T'Sergeant sent for a brew and a Rich-Tea or two
As the whole carry-on were revealed

S & S TREVITHICK *GENERAL STORE* PROV

Now Snowy, by the way, were called Colin
And to the Sergeant he had a bit banter
He said, "Right enough, I'm not from round here,
I'm from t'North pole, just nextdoor to Santa's"

It were the night before Christmas there's a knock on 'is door
And there stood a couple of elves
Sayin' "Santa wants to know if you'll come and help out?"
He says "Me? But I'm ten foot twelve"

They'd said "No, he doesn't want you for one of his elves,
He wants you to come guide the sleigh,
Poor Rudolph's in bed" "That's not like him" Colin said
"Goin' muckin' up Santa's big day"

"It weren't him it were Olive, the other reindeer,
She were laughin' and calling him names,
A big fight broke out and then she knocked him out,
For tryin' to join in wi' reindeer games"

So Colin the polar bear agreed right away
To help Santa out with his plight
And a few hours later he were heading the team
Of twelve reindeers as they up and took flight

He were a big lad were Col, they got done double quick
"There's just a few left" Santa said
But just as they flew over Amblethwaite zoo
Colin's eyes nearly popped out his head

It were the Polar Bear sign that like knocked him off line
And a swimming pool, looked flippin' fantastic
There were even a good looking female sat there
On an iceberg that were made out of plastic

So he'd a quick word wi' Santa and said "D'you mind,
If instead of going home, I stopped here?"
Santa just sniggered and said "That was me plan,
I got this letter and I had an idea"

"It were from that lassie sat sittin on th'iceberg,
She din't want a doll or a pup,
All she wanted were a boyfriend for Christmas,
And you're far too big to wrap up!"

Wally Kerr And The
Ghost Of Christmas Past

Poor Wally Kerr for Christmas each year
Got aftershave and posh smelly stuff
All the hints that he dropped did nothing to stop
Friends an' family knowin' 'nough were enough

He said "I'll not need any aftershave next year, Our Mam,
I think I've sufficient to last"
Cos it stared out 'is bathroom cabinet
Like the ghost of Christmas Past

It had the bathroom windowsill right chocker-block
No room for anything more
On the top of the cistern and all round the bath
And in boxes all over the floor

His dressing table were covered wi' Aramis n'that
And in spite of the times he had said
About not needing any after shave ever again
He had three crates of Brut 'neath the bed

He got the gift packs, the ones with the bath cubes
The shower gel and cissy shampoo
The foot powder, talc and the soap on a rope
The mouthwash and suppositories too

"Are you trying to tell me summat, or what?
Wi' all these pongy cosmetics you keep gettin' us?
Get a strap for me watch or a bottle of Scotch,
Or a nice set of spanners next Christmas!"

Okay, so he used the deodorant once
He even used the hair lacquer twice
But din't know what to do wi' a half ton of talc
And a gallon of Old piggin' Spice

He'd wrap some up nice to give away the next year
But the rest it were drivin'im up t'wall
So he sneaked a big load to the W.I.
To put on their tombola stall

He used the shampoo for cleaning the carpets
And the shower gel to clean out the bath
And his drains smelt quite nice cos he used his Old-Spice
And the bath salts for scrubbing the path

He used hair oil for oiling his bike chain
And conditioner for cleaning the bog
He used spray-on deodorant for the killing of flies
And the face-wash for washing his dog

So he decided he'd write off to Santa this year
And he wrote it all down in large print
Which he left lying round in the hope it were found
So's his family might just get the hint

It read "Dear Santa Claus, when you go to the stores,
To sort out this year's Christmas box,
I don't want Hai-Karate or Paco Rabane,
And for hell's sake, I don't need no socks!"

The Plight Of The Phoenix

One day quite by chance, Joe the plumber's wife, Nance
Saw two parrots in t'cage in a shop
She thought "Hey, they look nice, an' they're not a bad price"
So she nipped in and bought up the lot

But the next Monday night, she noticed summat not right
They were just sat there like two pounds of tripe
She said "Ello buggerlugs" but none of 'em budged
Till she prodded 'em wi' a bit of lead pipe

She muttered a curse, as they fell off the perch
Bein' alert, she thought "Summat's awry"
So she did t'best she could, force feedin' 'em grub
And chuckin' them to get 'em to fly

They wouldn't do nowt, they just laid there flat out
So she rummaged around for a box
"It's not on, isn't this" she says, getting' right miffed
And she took 'em both back to the shop

She says "I bought these two birds on August the third"
He said "Aye, so big deal. What's the prob?"
She says "There's summat not reet, they won't even eat,
I've had to shove t'seed in their gobs"

Then she opened the box and tipped them both out
She says "Just look at the state of the things,
They've both gone right limp and they're startin' to stink"
And she dangled them both by their wings

"I want 'em replaced" she said, stoney-faced
"A lifetime's guarantee's what you said"
"That's null and void" …She said "Why?" right annoyed
He said "Can't you see? You daft bugger, they're dead!"

She let fly with her bag and she clouted the lad
She said "Hey, watch your tongue. Where's yer manners?"
As he crumpled and sagged, she looked at her bag
And realised it was Joe's bag of spanners

He got up off the floor, sayin' "Don't hit us no more"
Quite shaken from Nancy's attack
But he soon changed his tune as he stood there and swooned
And says "I'll see what we've got out the back"

He were back in a jiff, he says "How's about this?"
He'd a strange looking bird on his arm
"I'd forgot it" he said "It lives in me shed,
Be careful" he said "It's quite warm"

"It's a phoenix" he told her "And sometimes they smoulder,
Here, have a feel of the heat"
She held out her hand, she said " Eeh, that feels grand,
I can train it to lie on me feet"

He were dead chuffed to get shot, were the bloke, like as not
It'd cost him a fortune you see
Settin' fire to his profits, burnin' holes in his pockets
He thought "She'll not get the better of me"

Next day she were back, she says "Hey, what's the crack?
It were sat on me shoulder last night,
Then it burst into flames, I've brought its remains,
And it's singed all me hair on the right"

So she tips up the box and the phoenix pops out
And starts shaking the ash from 'is wings
The bloke he just laughed "Yer guarantee's still intact,
They go on for ever these things"

Well it scorched all her curtains, burnt holes in t'settee
And the bog rolls in t'privy that night
Charred the banister rail, and singed the cats tail
Before setting the mattress alight

At church, Sunday morn, she sat next to Sid Vaughan
From the Crem, he were wringin' 'is hands
"Please God" he said "Forget daily bread,
A few tons of coke'd be grand"

She put a hand on 'is shoulder and Sid turned and told her
"I've got this big problem at Crem,
There's nowt I can do, there's three off with the flu,
And the coalman's not turned up again"

She says "Haven't you heard? I've got this rare bird,
It just bursts into flames – it's a winner"
He said "We'd a turkey like that, the Christmas just past,
So we had to have Spam for us dinner"

So he gave it a test, he said "Wow, I'm impressed,
It'll save us a fortune on coal,
But the furnace room blokes'll all go for me throat,
When I tell them they're back on the dole"

So it turned out quite well, as I'm sure you can tell
And the phoenix were chuffed with his plight
The Crem saved a few bob and gave Nancy a job
With an 'osepipe, 'case the place caught alight